RECYCLING THE PAST

Thomas J. Knock

Bruce Kuklick

John P. McWilliams, Jr.

Thomas H. Pauly

Thomas P. Riggio

Richard M. Rollins

Joan Shelley Rubin

RECYCLING THE PAST

Popular Uses of American History

EDITED BY

LEILA ZENDERLAND

 University of Pennsylvania Press/1978

Library of Congress Cataloging in Publication Data
Main entry under title:

Recycling the past.

    Includes bibliographical references.
    1.   United States—Intellectual life—Addresses, essays, lectures. 2. American literature—History and criticism—Addresses, essays, lectures. I. Knock, Thomas J. II. Zenderland, Leila.
E167.1.R434   973   77-20306
ISBN 0-8122-7740-6

CONTENTS

INTRODUCTION: USES OF THE PAST   vii
  Leila Zenderland

FICTIONS OF MERRY MOUNT   1
  John P. McWilliams, Jr.

IN SEARCH OF "THE SPIRIT OF '76"   29
  Thomas H. Pauly

WORDS AS SOCIAL CONTROL: NOAH WEBSTER AND THE
CREATION OF THE AMERICAN DICTIONARY   50
  Richard M. Rollins

UNCLE TOM RECONSTRUCTED: A NEGLECTED CHAPTER
IN THE HISTORY OF A BOOK   66
  Thomas P. Riggio

CONSTANCE ROURKE IN CONTEXT: THE USES OF MYTH   81
  Joan Shelley Rubin

"HISTORY WITH LIGHTNING":
THE FORGOTTEN FILM *WILSON*   95
  Thomas J. Knock

TRADITION AND DIPLOMATIC TALENT:
THE CASE OF THE COLD WARRIORS   116
  Bruce Kuklick

CONTRIBUTORS   133

INTRODUCTION

LEILA ZENDERLAND

In January 1977, over 130 million people witnessed the results of one American's search for a usable past. The commercial success of Alex Haley's book and television drama, *Roots,* surpassed the expectations of even its most optimistic promoters. For eight days, the nation followed "the saga of an American family" from slavery to freedom. Patrons in Harlem bars watched in silence; they refused to allow juke box music to break the spell even after episodes had ended. White viewers claimed to be seeing "black through different eyes." Some black leaders even spoke of the series as "the most significant civil rights event since the Selma-to-Montgomery march of 1965."[1] The phenomenon left media experts puzzled: why did an account of a slave family's experiences from 1750 to 1870 speak so powerfully to black and white Americans of the 1970s?

Historians may have some clues to the answer, for they have long been aware of the power and the purposes of rewriting history. Haley's title suggests that present behavior is grounded in past experience. Historiography also records the converse: the concerns of the present often necessitate a reconsideration of the past. Thus Charles Beard addressed his twentieth-century contemporaries by scrutinizing the finances of the founding fathers; and both Ulrich Phillips and W.E.B. Du Bois knew that interpretations of slavery and Reconstruction were critical for defending or denouncing the status quo. Yet Haley was not writing to correct the accounts of other historians. His work makes sense within another historiographic context: the past put to use by nonhistorians.

The essays collected in this volume all explore the ways that Americans other than historians have used experiences from the past. By examining sources ranging from the American dictionary to diplomatic memoirs, they

---

[1] Roger Wilkins, "The Black Ghosts of History," *New York Times,* Feb. 2, 1977, p. 22.

seek to show just how we have made aspects of our heritage work for us, how we have suborned ghosts from every corner of our history. Each essay reveals the ideas and artifacts of one era reemerging to answer the needs of another. The Americans discussed here—Noah Webster, Nathaniel Hawthorne, Thomas Dixon, Constance Rourke, William Carlos Williams, Darryl F. Zanuck, Dean Rusk—all used historical materials to speak to contemporary concerns. And just as the decade of the 1970s found its hero in an angry black slave, these people also found meaning in heroes out-of-context, in historical events misplaced: the spirit of 1776 in the marketplace of 1876; Uncle Tom in the Jim Crow South of 1900; Puritans in the Freudian art of the 1920s; Woodrow Wilson at the end of World War II; Munich in Vietnam.

In a sense these essays carry on the important myth-symbol scholarship in American Studies of Henry Nash Smith and Leo Marx. The contributors are interested in the myths Americans have had of their traditions and the historical symbols manifest in contemporary life. But the proponents of myth-symbol scholarship have tended to concentrate on works of literature only—and often literary classics—to make general claims about all of American culture and its mythic structure from the seventeenth to the twentieth century. The writers in this collection, on the contrary, are interested not in generating broad hypotheses but in seeing how specific ideas about the past function for limited groups of Americans in particular situations. Moreover, by considering both popular and great literature, film, advertising, and works of scholarship, these seven case studies afford us a closer look at the ways we use images of the past to address the present.

The essays collected here suggest at least four such uses Americans have made of their heritage. One obvious strategy is evident on advertisements, on product labels, or in the sale of historical souvenirs: businessmen use American history to sell products. America's entertainment industry endlessly reconstructs the past to capture audience interest and thus earn profits. The audience may also be using the past in a second sense: American history can be an emotional prop for individuals unsure of their own identity. Such reconstructions suggest what their "Americanism" might mean. Politicians derive additional meaning from the past by using the "lessons of history" to assess political alternatives and their consequences. In recent years, these "lessons" have become crucial in shaping United States foreign policy. Finally, the past provides an open-ended source of material for intellectual and artistic expression. Literary critics have long recognized that without a body of historic traditions, writers would be working in a cultural vacuum. These essays then allow us to explore in detail how Americans construed their history as a commercial venture, an emotional resource, a political tool, and an inexhaustible target of the intellect.

* * *

Any consideration of the uses of the past in America must take into account the American economy. Advertising, marketing psychology, and techniques of mass distribution affect the popularity of any product. Clever entrepreneurs have often found an abundance of ideas and materials in American history. Best-selling novels, popular films, and television series adapt historical themes—the "wild west," the gangster wars of the 1920s, the Depression, World War II, and most recently, the 1950s—to entertain audiences and to earn money for publishers, studios, and sponsors. Even the experiences of American prisoners of war in Nazi Germany have provided weekly comic fare. Commercials use historical motifs as well: old Quakers sell oatmeal, log cabins sell syrup, "great American homes" such as Monticello sell paint.

Thomas H. Pauly's essay in this volume explores this relationship between objects depicting American history and the contemporary marketplace by tracing the history of the most overused symbol of the Bicentennial, the trio of revolutionary musicians from the picture known as "The Spirit of '76." This picture is so familiar that the American public recognizes it even when the revolutionaries are played by three salesgirls renting cars, puppets promoting children's television, or costumed cows selling milk. Yet few Americans know the name of the artist who created the original or how it gained such fame. By following the work first known as "Yankee Doodle" from its beginnings as a chromolithograph sold at the Centennial Exhibition of 1876, Pauly finds modern usage to be an appropriate tribute to a work that immortalized the spirit of the industrial revolution more than any other.

Pauly credits the picture's fame not to its painter, Archibald M. Willard, but to its promoter, James F. Ryder, an entrepreneur who combined low prices with lavish publicity to produce a commercial, if not an artistic, masterpiece. "The Spirit of '76" survived while thousands of contemporary works judged superior by artistic standards faded away because Ryder understood the trends that were beginning to shape the art market: the decline of traditional oil painting and the rise of commercial illustration, the impact of photography, and the techniques of cheap reproduction. By dispelling the legends surrounding the picture's history, Pauly has uncovered a fitting symbol for America during the Centennial Era; while its subject matter glorified the past, its promotion embodied the values of industrial capitalism that would distinguish the second century of the nation's history from the first.

Pauly's essay suggests another aspect of the historiography of usage: the reappearance of Willard's picture, once established as a symbol of the nation's "spirit," during times of national pride. The ubiquitous musicians led the American army into Havana in 1898 and into Paris in 1917. In this context, the Bicentennial becomes the latest example of what Willard called "Yankee Doodle Times."

The selling of the past extends into other media as well. Thomas J. Knock discusses Darryl F. Zanuck's film *Wilson* and its massive publicity campaign designed to recoup the five million dollars that Twentieth Century-Fox had invested in the movie. Although its contribution to the selling of American internationalism was its most important aspect, the film was also a work of entertainment, designed to draw as many people as possible into the theatre. In its day, critics compared *Wilson* to *Birth of a Nation* and *Gone With the Wind,* praising it for advancing film's potential as an art form. The comparison is significant in another sense: both *Birth of a Nation* and *Gone With the Wind* also dealt with historical themes, translating the South's Civil War failure into box-office success. Yet these film classics began with an advantage over *Wilson.* Their stories had already proven commercially successful as best-selling fiction. *Birth of a Nation* adapted Thomas Dixon's popular novel, *The Clansman,* the first part of his trilogy on the Reconstructed South. *The Leopard's Spots,* the second volume of Dixon's trilogy, sold over a million copies alone, and helped to establish the publishing house of Doubleday, Page. Thomas P. Riggio's essay on *"Uncle Tom* Reconstructed: The Forgotten Chapter in the History of a Book" examines the reasons for Dixon's popularity.

Pauly, Knock, and Riggio show historical events shaped by an artist, a filmmaker, and a novelist, respectively, and produced as commercial ventures. Each demonstrates a relationship between economic structures and the dissemination of ideas. Together they provide evidence for an aspect of American culture that historians often overlook: the search for a marketable past.

Understanding why the public responds to such marketing strategies suggests a more general connection between America's heritage and the psyche of her inhabitants. Social psychologists have often explored this connection in attempting to define an "American identity," and to explain how it affects behavior. The problem has a long history: identifying an American has troubled writers since the time of Crèvecoeur, and historians have found the concept vague yet important in explaining the shift in loyalties away from Britain in the eighteenth century, the strength of sectionalism in the nineteenth century, and the "Americanization" of immigrants in the twentieth century. Recent concern over the meaning of American ethnicity suggests that the subject has not been laid to rest. Several essays in this volume show insecure individuals using the past to deal with what David Potter called their "compulsive preoccupation with the question of their Americanism."[2]

This preoccupation was most evident during the early national period, when Americans hastened to develop the necessary symbols of statehood. With the Fourth of July and the Star Spangled Banner, historians usually cite Noah Webster's *American Dictionary of the English Language* as an example of rising nationalism. Richard M. Rollins' study, "Words as Social Control: Noah Webster and the Creation of the *American Dictionary,*" revises this simple explanation in light of the ideologies competing to mold early American character. By paying strict attention to Webster's definitions, Rollins uncovers not a patriot of the 1780s but a frightened federalist of the 1820s concerned lest the forces of nineteenth-century democracy unleash chaos. Webster took refuge in a language that would impress upon all who used it the responsibilities of citizenship in the new American republic. Rollins proves that Webster's objective in devoting his life to a dictionary was not to distinguish American speech from British speech, despite his title, but to define how a true American should behave. Recognizing the power of definitions in any debate, Webster infused his American language with the quiet Christian virtues of obedience and duty that he hoped would stabilize the country. Through his dictionary, Noah Webster transformed events of the eighteenth century into rules of behavior for the nineteenth century.

Even as Webster wrote, a schism in the meaning of "Americanism" was moving the nation towards civil war. In the aftermath of their defeat Southerners too found consolation in returning to a past of their own construction. In *"Uncle Tom* Reconstructed," Thomas Riggio shows how Southern popular fiction directly contested the Northern image of the South embodied in *Uncle Tom's Cabin.* Harriet Beecher Stowe's book remained a powerful indictment of Southern society long after the Civil War had ended; Southerners responded by modifying the characters of Uncle Tom and Simon Legree to fit their own images of good and evil, as well as to answer the "Negro Question." Thus, New South spokesmen like Joel Chandler Harris and Thomas Nelson Page twisted Stowe's characters to present a paternalistic society of kindly slaveholders, villainous overseers, and emasculated slaves. In this fiction, Uncle Tom became Uncle Remus. Thomas Dixon's work of the early twentieth century took this transforma-

[2] David Potter, "The Quest for the National Character," in John Higham, ed., *The Reconstruction of American History* (New York: Harper and Row, 1962), 197.

tion one step further: Uncle Tom was now Tom Camp, a saintly poor white who hated the blacks. Dixon's fiction incorporated the ideology of his age, portraying blacks as beasts and Legree as a Northern capitalist mill owner. By this time, the "Negro Question" had become a national concern, and Dixon found a receptive Northern audience fearful of "inferior" immigration and capitalist expansion.

The past becomes much more than an emotional prop when it is used by politicians to justify present policies. When Lincoln began his Gettysburg Address by reminding his audience of what "our forefathers" had done "four score and seven years ago," he was invoking a powerful resource to defend his war for union. In fact, politicians have rarely explained America's wars in terms of expedience: whether the fight was to secure our "Manifest Destiny" or to "Make the World Safe for Democracy," the rhetoric of war has always made use of the broader themes of American history. Incidents from the past have equipped policy makers with the weapons for semantic warfare as well: just as federalist Noah Webster defined "democrat" as "synonymous with *Jacobian* in France . . .," a word hardly value-free in the early nineteenth century, defenders of American involvement in Vietnam labelled their opponents "appeasers." Knock's essay, " 'History with Lightning': The Forgotten Film *Wilson,"* and Bruce Kuklick's essay on "Tradition and Diplomatic Talent" show how Americans called upon the past to promote the peace effort in 1945 and to maintain the war effort in Vietnam. Defenders of both policies used the "lessons of history" to support their positions.

Kuklick analyzes the nature of such "learning from the past" by examining how diplomatic traditions emerge, gain acceptance, and eventually are supplanted. He shows how diplomats groomed under Woodrow Wilson came to power during World War II and shaped American international policy in the postwar years. For these men, Wilson's prophecy had been realized: America's failure to enter the League of Nations had precipitated a second world war. The country could not afford to repeat this historic "mistake." Kuklick explains how the "lessons of the 1930s" and especially the Munich analogy instructed policy makers of the forties, fifties, and sixties. Presidents Truman, Eisenhower, Kennedy, and Johnson all used this "central lesson of our time"—that unchecked aggression ultimately leads to war—to defend American foreign policy in Korea, West Berlin, Cuba, and South Vietnam. Kuklick is not interested in evaluating the truthfulness of such arguments; instead, he proposes an alternative way to examine this rhetoric by tracing how complex historic situations become crystallized into easily applied lessons.

Perhaps one such "lesson" to come out of the Vietnam war will be that winning public support can be critical to the success or failure of American foreign policy. Thomas Knock shows how a popular movie helped turn the tide of public opinion away from isolationism and towards internationalism in the mid-1940s. Darryl F. Zanuck's film interpretation of Wilson blended Ray Stannard Baker's biography, the memoirs of Mrs. Wilson and Henry Cabot Lodge, and the technical sophistication of Hollywood to depict Wilson at Princeton, in the White House, triumphant in Europe, and defeated at home. The timing of Zanuck's film (1944) left no doubts about its political significance. The film drew editorial praise as well as rave reviews from America's most important magazines and newspapers, and the controversies surrounding the film as fourth term propaganda for "Franklin Delano Wilson" brought it to the attention of Congress as well.

The most explicit recognition of the usefulness of the past has come neither from politicians nor from businessmen, however, but from America's intellectuals. Henry James expressed the longing for a usable heritage when he described the difficulties that Hawthorne had faced writing literature in a society with "no sovereign, no court, no personal loyalty, no aristocracy, no church . . . no Oxford nor Eton nor Harrow . . . no sporting class—no Epsom nor Ascot!"[3] Other intellectuals felt equally uncomfortable about being what Henry Steele Commager called "historical nouveaux riches."[4] In response, nineteenth-century writers tried to shape American materials into a body of literature to rival that of Europe, and to thus make America culturally self-sufficient. But literary nationalism reveals only half the problem: the man of letters struggling to survive in nineteenth-century America needed material as well as intellectual sustenance; he received little of either in an active society that placed a small premium on critical reflection. Intellectuals of the early twentieth century such as Van Wyck Brooks, disgusted by American cultural complacency, boldly called for a trenchant criticism of all aspects of American society. In doing so, they defined a new role for the American man of letters. Yet even these men acknowledged the critic's dependence upon a rich heritage worthy of explication; Brooks asked his readers to "discover, invent a usable past."

Joan Shelley Rubin explains Constance Rourke's work in the context of such anxiety over the role of the intellectual in America. By retrieving and embellishing America's early tall tales, Rourke thought she had found what Brooks and others were looking for: a "national fabric of spiritual

---

[3] Henry James, as cited in Henry Steele Commager, *The Search for a Usable Past* (New York: Knopf, 1967), 5.
[4] Ibid.

experience." Blending fact with fantasy in her biographies, Rourke created "legendary figures" large enough to embody the nation. She wanted her loosely defined "myths" to link America's folk culture with its serious literature, thus creating a new art form that would appeal to both high-brows and lowbrows. In this way, a critic would unite the American people.

Rubin shows Rourke's responsiveness to other intellectual currents of her day. Thus, Rourke applied anthropologist Ruth Benedict's conclusions about cultural uniqueness to avoid disparaging comparisons between American and European accomplishments. She learned from Jane Ellen Harrison's study of ancient Greek art and ritual that rudimentary art forms reveal the primitive rituals unifying a society; Rourke found America's "primitive elements" in native art forms such as the minstrel show. Yet Rourke's defense of America's heritage contained its own paradox: while she praised American art forms, Rourke also excused them as the products of a "prolonged cultural childhood." For Rourke, the past filled an emotional as well as an intellectual void; her sense of isolation intensified her desire to create an important role for Americans like herself. Rourke's understanding of how the past could be used to shape that role placed her at the center of the cultural concerns of her time.

In "The Fictions of Merrymount," John P. McWilliams, Jr. suggests that cultural critics may have underestimated the ability of creative artists to shape whatever episodes of American history are available. Despite Henry James' warning that it takes a great deal of history to produce a little literature, the fictions of Merrymount show how writers have transformed a minor historical incident into a sizeable literary repertory—romance, psychological fiction, poetry, librettos, and plays. The seventeenth-century skirmishes in which Puritans repeatedly suppressed opportunist Thomas Morton's settlement at Merrymount are politically insignificant. Historians treating the event have been frustrated by the conflicting partisan accounts of Bradford and Morton, and by the lack of evidence surrounding the controversial charges: gun sales to the Indians, miscegenation, and usurpation of legal authority. Yet, precisely because the details remain blurred, American imaginations have found room for meaningful reconstruction.

The conflict at Merrymount shows the past providing a focus for issues of contemporary moral and intellectual significance. Nathaniel Hawthorne saw in Merrymount a psychological and ethical battle: "jollity and gloom" were "contending for an empire." His contemporary, John Motley, voiced other concerns of an expanding mid-century America: Merrymounters, nostalgically looking back to Old England, were overpowered by the narrow-minded purposefulness of the Puritans, bearers of progress. In the wake of the Freudian revolution, twentieth-century Americans like William

Carlos Williams and Richard Stokes pitted Morton's frank recognition of sexual desires against a hateful Puritan repression. Two interpretations use Merrymount to consider the nature of history: Stephen Vincent Benet describes a benign American heritage generous enough to include deviants (like Morton) in retrospect; Robert Lowell, writing during the Vietnam War, instead sees a malevolent historical determinism at work, damning the victors as well as the victims.

Interestingly, the challenge of reconstructing an incident like Merrymount lies not in plot but in character depiction: Merrymount provides the chance to describe America's heroes and villains. Even the original records show the inclination towards caricature by both sides: to Morton, Bradford is an "elephant of wit"; to Bradford, Morton is a "mad bacchanalian." Those sticking closest to the historical records have found a creative tension in what McWilliams describes as the "patriotic demand to disparage an engaging reprobate." In the hands of later interpreters, Morton is variously a merry sinner, a vulgar royalist, an effete cavalier, or a persecuted advocate of free love. The Puritans, represented by Bradford or Endicott, are subject to even more manipulations, depending on whether the author wants to sanctify or calumniate the founding fathers. In their most recent reincarnation (1965), Morton is a disillusioned pragmatist struggling to survive, while Puritan Endicott is a "fascist turned existentialist" military leader.

McWilliams' Merrymount is a cultural Rorschach test, recording the hopes and fears of each generation. It offers scholar-critics a chance to explore in microcosm the broader themes of American history: the psychology of American guilt and innocence, the wilderness undermining the commandment to build a New Jerusalem, and the ambivalence about the course of American empire and the character of its builders. It proves the possibility of using parts of the American past to undertake the critical examination of American values demanded by twentieth-century intellectuals.

*   *   *

The subjects of these essays reflect some of the staple elements in our historical symbolizing: the founding of New England (Merrymount) and the Revolution (The Spirit of '76); the Jacksonian period (Noah Webster) and the Civil War and Reconstruction (*Uncle Tom's Cabin*); the intellectual awakening of modernism (Constance Rourke) and postwar internationalism (Wilson and the Cold Warriors). Examining when and why each of these symbolic episodes reemerges is also suggestive. Thus, the tale of Merrymount, as McWilliams indicates, has been popular for a long time, but as an example of "Puritanism," it became especially meaningful in the 1920s, when many intellectuals accepted Freud's theories justifying the pursuit of pleasure and were themselves discovering the hedonism that made Morton famous. The American Revolution too has always been a staple of our common history, but "The Spirit of '76" shows that popular consciousness was raised during the Centennial period (and again during the Bicentennial), in part because of the astute use of advertising in a technological society. Rollins' essay on Webster essentially tells us about a recurring concern in this country—the corruption of the Republic. Rollins shows how nineteenth-century evangelical Christians, fearful of egalitarianism, turned to nationalism as a conservative force. Riggio's essay on Uncle Tom suggests that a particular myth of the South was especially useful in maintaining racism long after the Civil War had ended; the fight against racism in contemporary America involved reconceptualizing slavery and Reconstruction once again.

"Constance Rourke in Context" shows a writer of the 1920s struggling to find and give shape to America's "mythic" folk tales. As many historians have observed, in the years following the First World War, American intellectuals first became critically distinct from their culture, conscious of the relativity of social knowledge and the precariousness of their place in the scheme of things. Rubin's essay then marks the time in which the very concerns of this collection of essays became a part of our culture. Rubin's Rourke exemplifies what has since become a social type: the semi-alienated intellectual desperately in need of certainty about her heritage but also convinced that her heritage is her own construct.

The articles by Knock and Kuklick take up recent and even contemporary events. Both authors discern that the rigors of internationalism needed an historical and ideological justification. *"Wilson"* shows how this justification was disseminated to American culture as a whole. "Tradition and Diplomatic Talent" delineates how it was more articulately worked out within the diplomatic community. Both point out that a culture-wide symbolic structure may grow out of immediately preceding events.

Collectively these essays demonstrate that scholars are increasingly aware of the importance of the study of myth for students of the culture. They also demonstrate how myths have functioned in specific social contexts. By tracing popular versions of American history embodied in our art, literature, and political and commercial rhetoric back to their sources, these authors have uncovered a diverse group of Americans searching for their own usable past. In explaining why each searched and what each found, they suggest the contours of a workable American heritage.

FICTIONS OF MERRY MOUNT

JOHN P. McWILLIAMS, JR.

THE CULTURAL SIGNIFICANCE OF SUCH A POLITICALLY AND ECONOMICALLY ephemeral episode as Merry Mount can emerge only by studying the interface between historical event and literary recreation. From William Bradford to Robert Lowell, prominent historical writers have returned to Morton's short-lived plantation, finding within its small scope and tragicomic demise a symbolic conflict of great moment for the national future. When the literary reach of an incident so outlasts its effect upon past events, its matter has become the stuff of legend. Verifiable information about its episodes, no longer of much concern to a political historian, assumes significance to the seeker of cultural mythology. Because historical literature tends to reshape the legends it claims to preserve, changes entering into the substance of such legends can be measured only by returning to the earliest records in an attempt to recover, if not historical truth, at least the extant data of original disagreements. To discuss the content of historical literature without an accompanying study of its historical subject is thus to ignore its ultimate import.[1]

For literary recreators of Merry Mount, the pull of myth-making upon the past has proven irresistible. The controversy, arising at the very beginnings of American civilization, offered sharply contrasting personalities in direct, often violent confrontation. Post-Revolutionary Americans, self-conscious about their national identity and needing to create a history, saw in Merry Mount an opportunity for reflection on the origins of the national character. In the very same incidents, twentieth century writers have traced the beginnings of failure, decline, or betrayal. For-

---

[1] D. F. Connors' *Thomas Morton* (New York: Twayne, 1969), a critical study of the *New English Canaan* with prefatory biographical material, ends by mentioning later characterizations of Morton and contains a helpful bibliography. Richard Sterne's "Puritans at Merry Mount: Variations on a Theme," *American Quarterly*, 22 (Winter 1970), 846–58, provides suggestive comparisons among the chief literary renderings of the episode. Neither Connors nor Sterne, however, is concerned with the process and meaning of historical distortion.

tunately, the meaning of the conflict was ready for reshaping because its historical facts had been conveniently obscured. By writing the *New English Canaan* (1637) and *Of Plymouth Plantation* (1630–1657), Morton and Bradford had served as partisan historians of their mutual hostilities. From the outset, Merry Mount has provided the historical writer a mirror in which he could find confirmation for his own ethics, for the values of his class, or for assumptions widely shared in his region or generation. To follow Merry Mount from the accounts of Bradford and Morton, through historians' reconstructions, to historical literature, is to survey one of the adaptable legends by which a people continues to define itself. First, however, an attempt to clarify and to de-moralize the recoverable pieces of fact has become, after 350 years of name calling, essential.

*   *   *

When Captain Wollaston established a fur-trading plantation in 1625 near the present site of Quincy, his community was the second settlement along 3,000 miles of coastline north of the Hudson. Consisting of three or four proprietors and about forty indentured servants, Mount Wollaston was rightly perceived as a threatening enterprise by the group of Puritan Separatists at Plymouth, thirty miles southeast. Although the new community shared Plymouth's interest in the profits of the fur trade, Wollaston's settlers cared little for the Covenant of Grace, Christian Calling, a just price, or the relationship between divine and civil law. Nor did they share the Puritan response to the frontier. In their trading post upon a hill, they were to be diligent in worldly business, but not dead to the world, to accept the wilderness for use and pleasure, not simply to subdue the inner and outer savage.

Among Wollaston's proprietors was Thomas Morton, a self-proclaimed gentleman of middling substance, who had studied at the Inns of Court and had come to America after a controversial inheritance case in which he had been plaintiff, lawyer, and prospective beneficiary.[2] Fond of Ovid, Ben Jonson's plays, Rosa Solis, and falconry, Morton soon developed passions, varying in kind, for the beauty of his new surroundings. The coast of Massachusetts, Morton later wrote, always appeared to him to be "Natures Masterpeece," a "paradice" of fair meadows, crystal fountains, and overburdened grape vines. In Morton's verse prologue to the *New English Canaan,* however, his attitude had been somewhat more

[2] The little known of Morton's early life in England is fully treated by C. E. Banks, "Thomas Morton of Merry Mount," *Massachusetts Historical Society Proceedings,* 58 (1925), 147–93.

aggressive; he had likened the land to a "faire virgin . . . most fortunate when most enjoy'd."[3]

One year after settlement, while Wollaston was in Virginia selling the time of unneeded servants, Morton conceived a more efficient system for using the land. If the remaining indentured servants would throw out Wollaston's lieutenant, he (lawyer Morton) would free all from service, then accept them as economic and social equals in a fur trading partnership. This cheeky offer, readily accepted, showed financial vision. The new arrangement brought returns of 600–700% over the next four years, perhaps as much as 1,000 pounds per indentured servant. Not surprisingly, the population of Mount Wollaston grew quickly, and William Bradford was sure of the reason: "Morton would entertain any, how vile soever, and all the scume of the countrie, or any discontente, would flock to him from all places."[4]

Morton had demonstrated that money could be made by social leveling and free enterprise; soon he was to defy Puritan notions of moral conduct, publicly and perhaps intentionally. On May Day of 1627, he celebrated the growth of his community by "Revels and Merriment after the old English custome," welcoming all comers, red or white, to a barrel of beer, a case of spirits, pistol contests, and dancing to drums around an eighty-foot maypole (276–77). According to Morton, the festivities were pagan and innocent: "There was likewise a merry song made which . . . was sung with a Corus . . . and performed in a daunce, hand in hand about the Maypole, whiles one of the Company sung and filled out the good liquor, like gammedes [sic] and Jupiter" (279). As evidence of the "harmless mirth made by younge men" on this occasion, Morton quotes, from memory and after seven years, their drinking song, which concludes:

> Lasses in beaver coats come away,
> Ye shall be welcome to us night and day.
> So drink and be merry, merry, merry boyes
> Let all your delight be in the Hymens joyes.

Governor Bradford, who was not present at the celebration, agrees only that the festival was pagan:

> They fell to great licenciousness, and led a dissolute life, powering out themselves into all profaneness. And Morton became lord of misrule, and

[3] C. F. Adams, Jr., ed., *New English Canaan of Thomas Morton* (1883; rpt. New York: Burt Franklin, 1967), 180, 114. Later references by parentheses in the text.
[4] William Bradford, *History of Plymouth Plantation*, eds. W. C. Ford et al. (1912; rpt. New York: Russell and Russell, 1968), II, 54. Later parenthetical references are to the second volume.

maintained (as it were) a schoole of Athisme. . . . They allso set up a
May-pole, drinking and dancing aboute it many days togeather, inviting
the Indean women, for their consorts, dancing and frisking togither, (like
so many fairies, or furies rather,) and worse practices. As if they had
anew revived and celebrated the feasts of the Roman Goddes Flora, or the
beastly practieses of madd Bacchinalians (48).

Groping to define the precise category of immorality to which Morton
belongs, Bradford here adds one Old World term to another (pagan, Lord
of Misrule, Fairie, Fury), until he arrives at the beastly, mad Bacchan-
nalian, which appears to satisfy him because it subsumes the other four.
Among Morton's moral offenses his supposed atheism and suspected
cohabitation aroused more lasting hostility than his drinking, dancing, or Maypole. Summarizing Plymouth's complaints against Morton's
men in a letter, Bradford was to emphasize their "living without all fear
of God, or common honesty, some of them abusing the Indian women
most filthily, as it is notorious."[5]

The May Day festivities were held in order to celebrate both the coming
of spring and the renaming of the community. Morton had probably intended the words Merry Mount to imply that "this jollity would have
lasted ever."[6] The peculiarity of his spelling, however, may indicate a
desire to taunt the Puritans with intimations of his "worse practices."
Whenever Morton refers to his community, he uses the spelling "Ma-re,"
unitalicized; whenever he refers to the adjective meaning joyful, he spells
it "merry" or "merrie." Since the publication of *Three Episodes of
Massachusetts History* in 1892, historical writers have accepted Adams'
conclusion that Morton was simply engaging in "an appropriate as well
as a highly characteristic display of Latinity"—that is, Morton had in
mind the ablative of *mare* and the name meant "the hill by the sea."[7]
However, Morton consistently italicizes his Latin and rarely shows any
regard for inflected endings. The *O.E.D.* does not list a variant spelling
of "ma-re" meaning "merry," nor "mare" meaning "by the sea"; it does
list, between 1540 and 1637, eleven occurrences of "mare," a female

---

[5] William Bradford's letter book, *Collection Massachusetts Historical Society,*
series I, vol. 3, 62.
[6] *History of Plymouth Plantation,* II, 49.
[7] C. F. Adams, Jr., *Three Episodes of Massachusetts History* (1892; rpt. New
York: Russell and Russell, 1965), 176. L. S. Davidson's novel *The Disturber* (1964),
for example, portrays Morton announcing "We shall spell our name Mare Mount,
explaining it means 'mountain by the sea'" (New York: Macmillan, 1964), 20.
See also George F. Willison's *Saints and Strangers* (New York: Reynal and
Hitchcock, 1945), 276. Recently, Richard Slotkin has noted that the name "Ma-re
Mount" may have had multiple meanings; see *Regeneration Through Violence*
(Middletown, Conn.: Wesleyan Univ. Press, 1973), 61.

horse. By playing upon the double meaning of "mount" and the four-fold connotations of "mare" (joyful, Mother of Christ, to join in matrimony, a female horse), Morton may have hoped to provoke his Puritan neighbors in 1627, and to amuse his Anglican readers in 1637, with a compound title of almost unlimited suggestibility. It is also at least noteworthy that the only execution for a crime other than murder in seventeenth century Plymouth took place in 1642 when Governor Bradford hung Thomas Graunger of Duxbury for committing "bestiality" with a "mare," among other animals.[8]

Had Morton's supposed offenses been restricted to social leveling, atheism, and debauchery his presence might have been suffered for a number of years. Morton had discovered, however, that the Indians were increasingly reluctant to trade furs for cloth and beads, if guns or liquor were available. According to Bradford, Morton knew that liquor made Indians dependent upon the trader, while guns increased their fur take. Bradford and his citizenry, who were equally eager for pelts, but unwilling to trade guns for them, grew fearful that "gain thirstic murderers" like Morton were arming the "barbarous savages" for a genocidal war (54–55). Morton later admitted that he had sold liquor, but only to Sachems; he neither admitted nor denied the selling of guns.

Although Morton contended that the Separatists conspired against him because they wasted their time "envying the prosperity and hope of the Plantation at Ma-re Mount" (282), Bradford mentions only a 1622 royal proclamation against selling firearms to the Indians as legal grounds for his commencing hostilities. Two admonitory letters were sent from Plymouth, to which Morton replied, correctly according to Coke, that a king's proclamation did not have the force of law, and that Plymouth had no jurisdiction over Merry Mount. Persuasion having failed, Bradford applied force. Waiting until most of Morton's associates were gathering furs in Maine, Bradford sent eight men under Captain Miles Standish to subdue him. Bradford recalls that, although Morton threatened to shoot Standish in his tracks, his consorts were too "over armed with drinke" to load, lift or aim their guns properly (56). When Morton wrote his version of the affair, his strategy for defaming was, like Bradford's, to heap up Old World analogies. Whereas Bradford's analogies serve to condemn ungodliness, Morton's ridicule pretension through mock-heroics:

Captaine Shrimpe [Miles Standish], the first Captaine in the Land (as hee supposed,) . . . takes eight persons more to him and, (like the nine worthies

---

[8] G. D. Langdon, Jr., *Pilgrim Colony: A History of New Plymouth, 1620–1691* (New Haven: Yale Univ. Press, 1967), 64.

of New Canaan,) they embarque with preparation against Ma-re-Mount, where this Monster of a man, as theire phrase was, had his denne. . . . The nine worthies comming before the Denne of this seaven headed hydra . . . began, like Don quixote against the windmill, to beate a parly and to offer quarter, if mine Host would yield. . . . Mine host no sooner had set open the dore, and issued out, but instantly Captaine Shrimpe and the rest of the worthies stepped to him, layd hold of his armes, and had him down; and so eagerly was every man bent against him, (not regarding any agreement made with such a carnall man,) that they fell upon him as if they would have eaten him (285–87).

After taking Morton to Plymouth jail, Standish reportedly urged that he be summarily shot. Bradford's more temperate head prevailed and, after a month's exile on an uninhabited island in the harbor, Morton was shipped off to an English trial.

Bradford's decision to deport Morton to England was a tactical error. Morton was to be tried by the Council For New England for selling guns to the Indians, but the Governor of the Council was Sir Ferdinando Gorges, a friend of Laud, and an impoverished Anglican knight, who looked forward to being granted New England as his private fiefdom, purified of Puritans. In this situation Morton appears to have adopted a two-sided defensive strategy. By telling Gorges that his only crime had been to read the *Book of Common Prayer* to his devout partners, Morton was soon freed from trial. By then aiding Isaac Allerton, agent of the Plymouth Colony, in obtaining fur-trading rights on the Kennebec from Gorges, Morton purchased the good will of his Puritan captor.

In the fall of 1629, fifteen months after being deported from Plymouth, Morton returned, as Allerton's official scribe, and probably as Gorges' unofficial spy, to Plymouth. Governor Bradford, convinced that Morton was lodged in Allerton's house "as it were to nose them," soon forced him out of Plymouth, whereupon he returned "to his old nest" at Merry Mount (74).

During Morton's absence, his plantation had survived the most famous of attempts to subdue it. Shortly after arriving in New England, John Endicott left ill-fed and disease-ridden Salem, in autumn, in order to impress his authority upon the Merry Mounters. All that is known of his journey is a one-sentence comment by Bradford: "That worthy gentleman, Mr. John Indecott, . . . visiting those parts caused that Maypole to be cutt downe, and rebuked them for their profanness, and admonished them to looke there should be better walking" (49–50). The felling of the maypole, praised and denounced for centuries, was historically little more than a dramatic gesture of moral disapproval. By refusing or failing to take personally punitive measures, Endicott accomplished only one change. After agreeing to alter the amoral name of the plantation, Morton's followers waited until Endicott returned to Salem, then renamed their settlement Mount Dagon.

Shortly after Morton returned to his community, Endicott applied political pressure. Calling a meeting of all settlers within a two-hundred-mile area, Governor Endicott insisted that each subscribe to two articles: 1) "that in all causes, as well Ecclesiasticall as Politicall, wee should follow the rule of Gods word"; and 2) that all trade would be supervised by the Governor of Salem, who would allocate profits and fix wages. The sole source of information about this meeting, Thomas Morton, claims to have stood alone in rejecting both articles. Refusing to admit that Endicott (whom Morton calls "Littleworth" or "the Cowkeeper of Salem") had any jurisdiction over him, Morton agreed to yield jurisdiction provided "the rule of Gods word" prove "in nothing contrary or repugnant to the lawes of the kingdom of England" (304–08). Equally astute in defending his economic interest, Morton argued that the proposal for a state-controlled fur trade was only a screen for Endicott's incompetence, and a guarantee of communal inertia.

Persuasion and pressure having failed again, the Puritans again chose force. Endicott and Bradford sent a joint detachment of soldiers to Merry Mount with instructions which remain unknown. Morton, learning of their coming, buried all of the community's corn and powder, then hid with his followers in the woods until the frustrated soldiers left.

The arrival of the Massachusetts Bay Company's fleet in 1630 rendered Morton's strategy of legal acuity and mock innocence, backed up by defiance or hiding, quite useless. At the first meeting of Governor Winthrop's Court, the first order of business was to house the clergy and the second to order that Thomas Morton be apprehended. A prisoner at the next session, Morton was not allowed to plead his case, but was given a summary, if comparatively lenient, sentence. Morton was stocked, all his goods were seized and sold, and his plantation was "burnt downe to the ground" before his eyes. The offense listed in the court records is the "many wrongs" Morton had done, ironically, to the Indians. The only specific charge is the stealing of a canoe; no mention is made of Maypoles, atheism, freeing indentured servants, or selling guns.[9] According to Morton, Winthrop justified the proceedings before the assembled court by declaring "the habitation of the wicked should no longer appeare

---

[9] R. Shurtleff, ed., *Records of Massachusetts Bay* (Boston, 1853), I, 75. See also J. K. Hosmer, ed., *John Winthrop's Journal: 1630–1649* (New York: Barnes and Noble, 1959), I, 53.

in Israel" (311). Morton himself was again deported for an English trial. This time, Bradford, Dudley, Winthrop, and Winslow, surely recalling that selling guns had not offended the Council previously, all wrote letters accusing Morton of murder.

Winthrop's decision to deport Morton to England was a grave tactical error. By destroying Merry Mount yet extraditing its master, Winthrop had now provided Morton with plausible evidence to plead that he was a persecuted Anglican. Morton was promptly freed by Gorges, the charge of murder was dropped, and no evidence has ever surfaced to confirm it. For the next seven years, Morton promoted the policies of Gorges and Laud with great success. As Gorges' solicitor, Morton managed the repeal of the patent for the Massachusetts Bay Company, thus leaving Endicott and Winthrop without any legal title to their lands. Then he promoted the redeeding of all Massachusetts grants to members of the Council For New England. To create favorable public opinion for this forthcoming colonial revolution, Morton published the *New English Canaan,* packed it discriminately with fact, lie, and caricature, then dedicated it to the Lords of His Majesty's Privy Council. By the time Gorges was ready to embark as Governor General for new New England, Morton was planning to accompany him. In the meanwhile, Winthrop had spent six months readying Boston for war: John Endicott's typically dramatic and futile response had been to cut the red cross out of the British flag.

The empire of Sir Ferdinando Gorges, reduced to paper when its financial underwriter unexpectedly died, was wholly quashed by the Cromwellian Revolution. Shortly after 1640, Thomas Morton suddenly discovered that Puritanism was the true religion. Attaching himself to Alexander Rigby, wealthy member of the Long Parliament and a Colonel in Cromwell's army, Morton developed a predictable interest in Rigby's patent for lands in Maine, and in 1643 disembarked as Rigby's land agent in Plymouth. The extent of Morton's infamy is revealed in the reaction to this third return. Morton was over sixty years of age, too poor to buy wine, and without followers. When Bradford allowed Morton to remain in Plymouth until early spring, Standish protested vigorously, arguing that Morton be imprisoned because Morton's falcon had trespassed over Standish's property. Edward Winslow warned Governor Winthrop "this serpent . . . out of doubt in time will get strength to him if he be suffered."[10] And John Endicott, hearing that Morton might be coming north, also wrote to Winthrop, seeking military assistance because "it is most likely that Jesuits or some that way disposed have sent him

---

[10] *Collections Massachusetts Historical Society* (Boston, 1863), series 4, vol. VI, 175.

over to do us mischief, to raise up our enemies round about us both English and Indian."[11]

When evicted from Plymouth, Morton went to Maine and then to Rhode Island, probably to promote Rigby's land schemes, and surely to avoid the jurisdictions of Endicott and Winthrop. Where and how Morton was apprehended remains unknown, but by November of 1644 he was again in jail in Boston. This time Governor Winthrop did not repeat his tactical error of deporting Morton for English trial. He left Morton in prison while dispatching a Mr. Downing to England "to search out evidence against him."[12] When Morton petitioned for a hearing or a trial, Winthrop brought him before the Court of Assistants to report that Morton was suspected of two offenses: 1) He had made a "complaint against us" at the King's council nine years earlier; and 2) He had written a scurrilous book called the *New English Canaan*. Although these were not indictable crimes, such crimes might be forthcoming from England, whereupon a formal trial could be held. After remaining a year in jail, uncharged and untried, Thomas Morton, "being old and crazy," was released.[13] Winthrop fined him 100 pounds, charges unknown and payment impossible, then urged him to leave Massachusetts. He went to the vicinity of the Rigby patent in York, Maine, where he lived, apparently uneventfully, until his death in 1647. In his will, Thomas Morton "of Cliffords Inn gent." bequeathed 10,000 acres along the Connecticut River, 2,000 acres along Casco Bay, and the entire island of Martha's Vineyard to Tobias Milles and Sarah Bruce, widow, who never collected.[14]

No authoritative judgment of the Merry Mount controversy can be written until crucial evidence for major points of issue is recovered. The fundamental question of jurisdiction, for example, is hopelessly entangled. In the 1660s, Samuel Maverick asserted that Morton had held a patent for his land which preceded any patent held by Winthrop or Endicott[15]; no record of that patent has been found. Plymouth's jurisdiction over Merry Mount is also debatable, not only because Plymouth's original grant was for land in Virginia, but because the boundaries of the 1622 and 1629 grants were poorly defined.[16] Furthermore, even if Bradford's jurisdiction included Mount Wollaston, he may have arrested Morton for ignoring a dead proclamation, rather than breaking a law.

---

[11] L. S. Mayo, *John Endecott* (Cambridge: Harvard Univ. Press, 1936), 181.
[12] *Records of Massachusetts Bay*, II, 90.
[13] Hosmer, ed., *John Winthrop's Journal*, II, 194–96.
[14] C. E. Banks, "Thomas Morton of Merry Mount," 163.
[15] Undated letter of Samuel Maverick to the Earl of Clarendon, *New York Historical Society Collection*, 1869, 40.
[16] Langdon, *Pilgrim Colony*, 14, 17, 188–89.

There is no conclusive evidence that the Merry Mounters sold one gun to the Indians, slept with Indian women, or encouraged drunkenness and atheism. Conversely, Plymouth's authorities revealed no envy of Merry Mount's prosperity, nor did they prosecute Anglicans living outside town limits for reading the *Book of Common Prayer*. Bradford's one-sentence account of Endicott's cutting down the Maypole says nothing of Endicott's motives, his reception, or the consequences of any punishments. Merely skeletal information exists about the charges and proceedings of Morton's many court appearances on both sides of the Atlantic.

Historians have never recognized that the lack of evidence poses only minor problems compared to the problems of the existing evidence. Any attempt to decide an issue of the controversy leads one back to the shifting sands of the two major texts. If we leave aside the brief court records and a few extant letters, Morton's life and the events at Merry Mount must be reconstructed from Morton's *New English Canaan* and Bradford's *Of Plymouth Plantation*. Thus any historical judgment can be made only from the accounts of the two principal controversialists, both of whom wrote at least six years after the fact. In both works, versions of Morton and Merry Mount are created, not primarily to exonerate the author, and certainly not to satisfy the needs of objective historicism, but to dramatize a dead quarrel within the larger context of justifying the exodus of the Saints, or of promoting a resettlement by the Anglicans.

For these purposes, creation of character was more important than recall of fact. Neither Bradford nor Morton made efforts to record controversial episodes precisely as he remembered them, or even in chronological order. Neither determined which of the other's objectionable traits had aggravated dislike into action. Instead, they encouraged *a priori* notions of character to shape their recall of events. To Bradford, Thomas Morton represents ancient godlessness: precivilized, pagan, cunning in strategy but carnal in desire, equally heedless of racial distinctions, society's needs, and biblical morality. Bradford may show us Morton as a trader, celebrant, or politician, but Morton always acts as if he were Dionysus unleashed.

To Morton, William Bradford represents the absurd Separatist: lower class, clumsy, anti-intellectual and busily self-righteous, anxious to display his bogus purity by bursts of oppression. Morton's caricatures of Bradford, Endicott, Winthrop, and Standish seem to merge into one figure because each has served to introduce generalizations about the Puritan character. All Puritans are "elephants of wit" (312); all have "special gifts for envy and mallice" (339); all "wink when they pray, because they thinke themselves so perfect in the highe way to heaven that they can find it blindfould" (334). Morton, like Bradford, has relied upon a pre-formed character type, traits of which can always be extracted to explain troubling memories. Bradford's moments of hesitant lenience can be interpreted as bungling, Bradford's fear of armed Indians as financial envy, and Bradford's distaste for "Indian consorts" as a sign of prurience.

Since Bradford's death, American historians have shown precious little regard for the incompleteness and inconsistencies of the historical record. The *New English Canaan,* to be sure, was not readily available until 1838, yet no historian made any effort to incorporate Morton's book—or even the extant court records and letters—until the 1880s. Nathaniel Morton, Cotton Mather, Prince, Hutchinson, Felt, and Palfrey were all content to quote Bradford's account as the historical truth, without considering its date of composition, context in *Of Plymouth Plantation,* or the social ethics of the author.

Such a confusion of paraphrase with fact is, of course, predictable as well as revealing. Not only was Governor Bradford a founding father and national saint; the prevalent conception of American history as a record of Divine Providences for the saving remnant found its chief model in Bradford's work. These considerations alone, however, cannot explain the joyous venom of editorial comments added by historians to their redactions of Bradford. Quotations from three widely read histories of different centuries will suffice for examples. Nathaniel Morton (1669): "Wickedness was beginning, and would have further proceeded, had it not been prevented timely"; Cotton Mather (1702): "a plantation of rude, lewd, mad English people, who did propose to themselves a gainful trade with the Indians, but quickly came to nothing"; J. G. Palfrey (1858): "a rabble rout" who practiced "habits of shameless license and revelry—drunkenness, gambling, dancing about a maypole, singing ribald songs, debauching Indian women" led by "a vagabond, whose presence it was impossible to endure."[17] These are the comments of men whose senses of historical proportion and perspective have abandoned them. Perhaps the very shrillness of their condemnation reveals a fear that the practices of America's first counter culture might revive.

The passions Merry Mount can evoke have continued to retard disinterested scholarship. The best historical accounts of Morton and his community remain those of Charles Francis Adams, Jr.[18] Elder brother of

[17] Nathaniel Morton, *New England's Memorial* (Boston: Solomon Southwick, 1772), 80; Cotton Mather, *Magnalia* (New York: Russell and Russell, 1967), I, 59; John Gorham Palfrey, *History of New England* (New York: A.M.S. Press, 1966), I, 232–33.
[18] Adams' "Thomas Morton of Merrymount" (his preface to the *New English Canaan*) and *Three Episodes of Massachusetts History.*

Henry, and President of the Massachusetts Historical Society, Adams republished the *New English Canaan,* uncovered nearly all the additional source documents, and wrote the fullest account of Merry Mount yet to appear. Despite his discoveries, Adams' methods and reasoning show the loyalties his name and position suggest. He repeatedly dismisses or ignores Morton's account of crucial episodes, yet quotes Bradford's approvingly and in full.[19] Recognizing that the two court proceedings against Morton were legally questionable, Adams nonetheless justifies both of the sentences on grounds of "self-preservation."[20] While stating that there is no evidence for Morton's having committed murder, Adams also cautions that there is "nothing very improbable" in the charge. When Morton told Endicott he would obey only the King's law, Morton was merely attempting "to display his legal acumen." It is Adams' magisterial epithets, however, which fully reveal his biases: "A vulgar Royalist libertine," "a scoffer, a man of undevout mind," "a born Bohemian . . . without either morals or religion."[21] The kindest judgment Adams can muster is his condescendingly genteel compliment to the pageantry of Morton's May Day: "It was not a vulgar modern instance of the frontier dance hall; there was a certain distance, and grandeur and dignity about it—a majesty of solitude, a futurity of empire."[22]

Recently, editorializing about Morton within a careful scholarly and historical context has reached rather different conclusions. Richard Slotkin's *Regeneration Through Violence,* a lengthy study of American attitudes toward the frontier, understandably attributes generative importance to the conflict between Puritans and Merry Mounters. Slotkin's account, however, contains three distortions: Wollaston had "abandoned" his plantation to Morton; Plymouth's wrath fell upon Morton because of the May Day celebration; the selling of guns was a subsidiary, almost negligible issue. These warpings of fact induce Slotkin's reader to justify Morton's conduct and to accept a distorted summary of Morton's values. Although Morton had been fond of jibing that the Indian was more humane than the Christian, Morton had never, even remotely, suggested that Christendom could be regenerated by miscegenation and by tapping the sexual power of the natural life. Slotkin, however, makes Morton

---

[19] "Thomas Morton of Merrymount," 18, 25, 27–28, 44.

[20] Ibid., 27, 45. *Three Episodes,* 203, 244.

[21] Adams, "Thomas Morton of Merrymount," 5, 39, 92, 94, 96.

[22] Adams, *Three Episodes,* 182. In the next generation, even a widely read historian wary of Puritan sanctity could continue to find Morton irredeemable. After condemning Merry Mount's economic practices in *The Founding of New England* (Boston: Atlantic Monthly Press, 1921, p. 113), James Truslow Adams was to brand Morton a "worthless rake" in the *Dictionary of American Biography* (New York, 1934) VII, 267.

into a humorless prophet of late 1960s rhetoric: "In this union of Pagan Indian and Christian Englishman, Morton finds the hope of a great renewal of power, fervor and goodness in the religious and social life of the human race." Morton, who had admitted the self-interest of his commitments to profit and law, appears as a selfless philosopher offering a psychic panacea to white civilization: "Morton remains true to his major theme; that the Englishman must withhold nothing of himself from the wilderness and the Indian but merge thoroughly with them and refresh himself at the sources of human passions and affection."[23] These quotations are true neither to the tone, vocabulary, nor substance of the *New English Canaan.*

*   *   *

For post-Revolutionary New England writers of imaginative historical literature, Merry Mount posed a vexing problem. Like the romantic historians, they wished to see the pilgrims as humane ur-libertarians who in 1620 had planted seeds of democracy and toleration which would flower in 1776, thereby illustrating the universal law of progress toward republicanism.[24] A thorough study of Merry Mount's demise, however, might have led them to question whether the Puritan's treatment of Morton had been libertarian, humane, democratic, or tolerant. And yet, to ignore Morton was to slight a celebrated episode of regional history and to miss a splendid opportunity for romance. Moreover, the subject set obligation against inclination. The moral disapproval which Merry Mount was felt to deserve became increasingly qualified by a lingering over its gay sensualities, and by a growing admiration for Morton's personable, if not honorable, traits. Thus the need to canonize regional forefathers was checked both by an admirable desire for historical accuracy in historical romance, and by an increasingly explicit urge to question the perfection of the Saints.

In the 1820s, however, historical writers had devised new and additional means for vilifying Morton. Lydia Child's *Hobomok* (1824) asserts that "the thoughtless and dissipated Morton," motivated "partly from avarice and partly from revenge," had begun to sell rifles to Indians with the express intent of inciting a massacre of the pilgrims.[25] Not only did Merry Mount attract the "careless" and "profane" (82); Morton was personally responsible for the Pequot War (54). Three years later, Catharine Sedgwick developed a mere surmise of regional historians into an unquestioned conspiracy. In *Hope Leslie* (1827), Morton becomes

---

[23] Slotkin, *Regeneration Through Violence,* 60, 62.

[24] See George Bancroft, *History of the United States of America* (Boston: Little, Brown, 1834–1861), I, 310, 322, 463 and VII, 23, 384–403.

[25] Lydia Child, *Hobomok* (Boston: Cummings, Hilliard and Co., 1824), 37.

the "old friend and patron" as well as the "companion in excesses" of Sir Christopher Gardiner—land-hungry aristocrat, Royalist, Catholic, bigamist, murderer, pretended Puritan, and would-be rapist.[26] Gardiner has learned his treacherous villany by serving as the "protegé and ally of Thomas Morton, the old political enemy of the colony" (II, 272). Lest the reader imagine that Morton escaped his just reward, Sedgwick pictures him in a "miserable little squalid den" of Winthrop's jail. Ragged and fiery-eyed, bursting into "inarticulate chattering and laughing," Morton has become a "maniac" who leaps upon anyone entering his cell (II, 140–43).

The charge of direct complicity in the Gardiner conspiracy seemed the last nail in the coffin of Morton's reputation. It reduced the immorality of May Day and the danger of trading firearms to subsidiary measures in an unrelenting scheme to overthrow the very act of Puritan settlement, even before 1630. Although early association with Gardiner is the least provable of charges against Morton, it became one of the most familiar because Longfellow perpetuated it in *Tales of a Wayside Inn* (1863). Longfellow's penchant for prettifying legends did not dissuade him from firmly condemning "roystering Morton of Merry Mount/ That pettifogger from Furnival's Inn/Lord of Misrule and riot and sin,/Who looked on the wine when it was red."[27]

The extent of Morton's infamy during the antebellum years is suggested by the unacknowledged use which two major writers made of his book. To support the suggestion that Indians in their natural state might have possessed redeeming qualities, Washington Irving twice inserted lengthy passages from the *New English Canaan* into *The Sketch-Book,* yet refused to specify his authority beyond the phrases "an old historian of New England" and "an old record of the early settlement of Massachusetts."[28] Although Whittier's "The Bridal of Pennacock" (1844), a long verse narrative about Indian hospitality practices, derives its plot and many details from one of Morton's Indian anecdotes, Whittier cites his source only by a fleeting phrase in the headnote, "Vide Morton's New

---

[26] Catharine Sedgwick, *Hope Leslie* (1827; rpt. New York: Garrett Press, 1969) II, 42, 140.

[27] Longfellow, "The Rhyme of Sir Christopher," ("The Landlord's Tale") from *Tales of a Wayside Inn, Complete Poetical Works* (Cambridge: Houghton Mifflin, 1922), 284. In 1846 Alexander Young had declared the Gardiner–Morton conspiracy to have been a historical fact. See *Chronicles of the First Planters* (Boston: Little, Brown, 1846), 334–35.

[28] "Traits of Indian Character," in R. H. Stoddard, ed., *The Sketch-Book Works of Washington Irving* (New York: Co-operative Publication Society. 1900), I, 309, 311.

Canaan."[29] Such slights as these, designed to protect the authority of the writer's source, are different in kind from the convenient omission of Morton in Bancroft's *History*. Only by deliberate distortion could Winthrop's treatment of Morton be reconciled with characterizations of Puritans as founders of libertarian justice.

In spite of the continuing attacks upon Merry Mount by both regional historians and female novelists (perhaps because of them), Hawthorne was the first writer to define the psychological significance of the controversy, or to consider it in an equable tone. It was Hawthorne, not Cotton Mather or Palfrey, who first had the historical acuity and stylistic precision to state "the future complexion of New England was involved in this important quarrel."[30] In the confrontation between "the gay sinners" and "the grizzly saints," Hawthorne perceives that "jollity and gloom were contending for an empire" (54). By suggesting that more was at stake than matters of guns, race relations, jurisdiction, or the fur trade, Hawthorne brings out the undeclared issue beneath the hectoring of historians and earlier romancers.[31] His reader is encouraged to view the struggle over Merry Mount as the working out of a regional if not national character, of a common "complexion."

In Hawthorne's tale, the religious, economic, and racial dimensions of the historical controversy recede, to be replaced by a symbolic contrast of human psychology (jollity vs. gloom) and of social ethics (hedonism vs. asceticism). Unlike any predecessor, Hawthorne begins by encouraging his reader to appreciate the color, vibrancy, and gaiety of Merry Mount. These changes render the Puritans' destruction of the community swifter, more sadistic, less justifiable. Gloom, one might conclude, has regrettably won out over jollity, loveless duty over revelry, abstract principles over sensual response. By the end of the tale, however, Hawthorne has so altered and refined the reader's attitudes to Endicott and the

---

[29] Whittier, *Complete Poetical Works* (Cambridge: Houghton Mifflin, 1894), 23.

[30] Hawthorne, "The May-Pole of Merry Mount," in J. D. Crowley, ed., *Twice-Told Tales* (Columbus: Ohio State Univ. Press, 1974), 62.

[31] By borrowing the works of four annalists from the Salem Atheneum, Hawthorne had become thoroughly familiar with Bradford's account, yet made major changes which still await thorough study. Hawthorne's Puritans attack Morton's paganism and illusions, not his economic or sexual practices. No May Day festival had been occurring when John Endicott arrived at Merry Mount, nor is there evidence for the brutal punishment which Hawthorne's Endicott inflicts upon the celebrants. For Hawthorne's sources, see M. L. Kesselring, "Hawthorne's Reading: 1828–1850," *Bulletin of the New York Public Library*, 53 (1949), 55–71, 121–38, 173–94. Hawthorne's borrowings are discussed by G. H. Orians, "Hawthorne and 'The Maypole of Merry Mount,'" *Modern Language Notes*, 52 (1938), 159–67 and by N. F. Doubleday, *Hawthorne's Early Tales* (Durham: Duke Univ. Press, 1972), 92–101.

Merry Mounters that the words "jollity" and "gloom" seem simplistic. The maypole may appear to recall the Golden Age, but the celebrants are futilely trying to perpetuate lively Elizabethan customs in a new and barren world. Our appreciation of the visual beauties of the pageant is qualified by Hawthorne's reflections upon the actors. The maskers may be either "Gothic Monsters," freed to express sexual perversions, or fantasts acting out their "latest day dream" (55). Conversely, the Puritans, who had been introduced as "most dismal wretches" (60) substituting the whipping post for the maypole, gain a measure of respect and sympathy. Endicott, like the narrator, recognizes that Merry Mount's happiness is illusory; it is Endicott, not the Merry Mounters, whose heart is touched by the Lord and Lady of the May.

As the tale develops, happiness is increasingly dissociated from mirth, while love is associated with "earth's doom of care and sorrow" (58). A traditional interpretation of the story contends that Hawthorne added the fictional Lord and Lady of the May to the historical outline so that they might embody a *via media* which would be historically possible as well as ethically desirable. The truth of this view depends upon the reader's notion of the tale's subject. Hawthorne tells us in his introductory note that his tale is "a sort of allegory" (54). If Hawthorne intended one of his Allegories of the Heart, his ending is at least plausible. Edith and Edgar need represent only a timeless marriage of human love and sorrow, rather than the future youth of New England. Their feelings can be, as they apparently are, directed toward a solely heavenly future, and not toward regret for a paradise well lost.

If Hawthorne intended a historical allegory, his ending is curiously incomplete. The community of a John Endicott is not a place in which the sensitivity of Edith and Edgar could easily survive. Moreover, Merry Mount itself, Hawthorne reminds us, has utterly ceased to be. Thus Edith and Edgar can represent a *via media* for the human heart, but not for the "future complexion of New England." Hawthorne is unable to provide them an earthly seat or a historical future, and makes no attempt to do so. Although Endicott returns with all the Merry Mounters to Salem, Massachusetts, Hawthorne's last sentence states that the Lord and Lady of the May "went heavenward, supporting each other along the difficult path which it was their lot to tread, and never wasted one regretful thought on the vanities of Merry Mount" (62). Hawthorne's ending thus abandons the historical issues his story had set forth. Perhaps he had intended to justify a compromise of regional character for which he could find no historical basis. In other fictions, he was frequently to show that New England's second generation embodied the most gruesome of

Puritan traits. In 1629, the time of the Gray Champion had not yet arrived.

Unaware of Hawthorne's tale, but thoroughly familiar with the *New English Canaan* as well as the journals of Bradford and Winthrop, John Lothrop Motley completed his lengthy and ambitious *Merry Mount* in 1849. Whereas Hawthorne had called for a "philosophic romance" about Mount Wollaston, and then had written an allegorical tale, the interests of Motley's romance are solely and expectedly historical. Although Merry Mount is Motley's ostensible subject, his concern is the struggle of forces leading to settlement. His controlling purpose, he concludes, has been to awaken "a spark of sympathy for the heroic souls, who in sorrow and self-denial laid the foundation of this fair inheritance of ours."[32]

An endeavor of such ancestral piety promises historical distortions which Motley will not allow. He portrays Morton from his assumption of power at Merry Mount until his death in Maine with an admirable regard for the ambivalences of the historical record. Unlike earlier novels and later histories, Motley's romance allows Morton whatever merits might plausibly be inferred from written accounts. Morton is "eloquent, adroit, bold, good-humored" and no murderer (13); his appetites for money, liquor, and women are real but occasional, and indicate no lust for depravity. Repeatedly, Morton is shown to have the right of legal issues, including jurisdiction. After Standish apprehends Morton "without the slightest shadow of legitimate authority," Morton refrains from killing Standish because of innate "generosity" (61). Motley has endowed Morton with an irrepressible wit, a genuine gift for word play, which is historically probable and personally endearing.

Motley's Puritans no more qualify for sainthood than his Morton qualifies for villainy. As a class, the Puritans are judged to be "iron-handed, despotic, stern, truculent, bigoted religious enthusiasts" (235), men with no understanding of historical and moral complexity. When Motley quotes Bradford's most memorable slurs ("lascivious nest of unclean birds," "lord of misrule," "dancing and frisking together"), they are spoken by a literal-minded Puritan blockhead, Corporal Neegoose. It is Deputy Governor Dudley, a "bigoted and intolerant Calvinist" (176), who refers to Morton as a "graceless reveller" and a "lewd mischief maker" (104). The chapter dealing with Morton's trial in 1630 shows that Winthrop and Dudley condemned Morton unheard, then cruelly sentenced him on charges which were red herrings, because they falsely

---

[32] Motley, *Merry Mount: A Romance of the Massachusetts Colony* (Boston: James Munroe, 1849), II, 249. Page references are to the first volume unless otherwise noted.

suspected him of inciting an Indian uprising. Thus Morton seems quite right to assume that Puritans are "as wise as serpents, if not as harmless as doves" (II, 156).

By uncovering the questionable means used to suppress Morton, Motley's romance exposes the falsities of characterizing Puritans as ur-libertarians. Intolerant and oligarchic though the Puritans were, however, Motley ultimately prefers spiteful Calvinists to gay Merry Mounters. His handling of the May Day and arrest scenes dramatize his reasons. Morton arranges the revels for purposes of nostalgia, not debauchery. Intended to summon up "the stirring memories of brighter ages" (165), Morton's May Day is a potpourri of irrecoverable chivalric traditions, including quarter staff tourneys dedicated to King Arthur, and Milk Maid and Morris Dances presided over by Robin Hood (Morton) and by Maid Marian (a squaw). Morton concedes that in this barren desert, "he must even do his best with the materials which he can find" (165). Rather than deal with New England's trials as they are, Morton prefers to embrace illusion. His defense of the May Day festivities is characteristic: "What a forlorn and shivering chicken will poor humanity prove when they have plucked all the feathers out of its tail. A fig for life when it has lost its illusion. The foul fiend fly away with the world, for me, when it hath grown virtuous and sensible and regenerated" (165).

For Motley, the fundamental cause of Morton's downfall is his failure to plan and to act. On both occasions when Merry Mount degenerates into riot, Morton's unwillingness to control his animalistic followers by any means other than ridicule is responsible. Knowing that Winthrop's agents soon will arrest him, Morton spends his time enjoying the aesthetics of falconry "totally lost to everything in the world below" (II, 168). Throughout the novel, Morton's acts are defensive and his responses aristocratic. He restores medieval ceremonies, quotes Ovid and Horace, talks of his "suzerainty," and cites dead English laws. "A most unskillful general, and a most impolitic monarch" (II, 16), he will make no effort to acquire a deed, to plan a trading empire, or to arm his community. In characterizing Merry Mount, Motley thus chose to emphasize a historically minor matter, the fragility of its social customs, rather than the forward-looking free enterprise, if not capitalism, of its economic practices.

Like Catharine Sedgwick, Motley organizes his plot around the Gardiner conspiracy, but unlike her, he so carefully restricts the charge that he qualifies it out of existence. Although Morton "seemed" (14) or "was supposed to be engaged" (II, 15) in the Gardiner-Gorges plot as early as 1628, Morton proves to be of little or no service to the expectedly villainous Gardiner. The two are seen together on numerous occasions,

Morton is declared to be "Gardiner's chief confidant, ally, and instrument" (II, 89), yet their association is ultimately a means for Motley to credit Morton's decency, while pitying his inability to help himself. Despite many attempts, Gardiner never persuades Morton to devise a political policy. As early as 1628, Gardiner recognizes that Morton is too "reckless" to make an "excellent conspirator" (II, 90). When Gardiner swears to gain fiefdoms by wrecking the Puritan settlement, Morton calmly replies "I hardly sympathize with your ferocity" (II, 158). After Morton's second arrest and the discovery of Gardiner's scheme, Morton is seen reflecting upon the ruin of Gardiner's "airy castles . . . with something of a child's indifference at the ruin of a card palace" (II, 152). The analogy is telling; like Hawthorne, Motley views Merry Mount as a childish gesture which must inevitably be uprooted by men of energy.

However real Morton's supposed passivity may have been, it is essential to Motley's standards of historical judgment. Morton is not evil; he is simply, and somewhat regrettably, an anachronism, an embodiment of all those losing qualities summoned up by the word "cavalier."[33] When Henry Maudsley, nominal hero of the novel, first sees the Merry Mounters, he quizzically asks a conventional question of epic poetry: "Are these the men to found an empire? Are these the pioneers of civilization and Christianity in this benighted but virgin world?"(50). Puritan convert though Maudsley is, he first dismisses the May Day rites as antiques, then condemns their decadence as an afterthought: "It were a nobler destination for this stern and unappropriated wilderness, to become a new realm for earnest and self-sustained enthusiasts . . . than to fall under leaders . . . seeking only to transplant upon this wild territory the worn-out follies, the decrepit purposes, the reeking crimes of civilization" (175).

Whereas Morton represents the English past, the Puritan represents the American future. The very narrow-mindedness of the Puritan makes him active and purposeful; his harshness is his source of strength. Winning though Morton's wit may be, only the force of Puritan intolerance is sufficiently strong to settle the wilderness. Because the brutal self-reliance

[33] In "Main Street" (1849), Hawthorne characterizes Morton in strikingly similar terms: "And next, among these Puritans and Roundheads, we observe the very model of a Cavalier, with the curling lovelock, the fantastically trimmed beard, the embroidery, the ornamented rapier, the gilded dagger, and all other foppishnesses that distinguished the wild gallants who rode headlong to their overthrow in the cause of King Charles. This is Morton of Merry Mount" (J. D. Crowley, ed., *The Snow-Image* [Columbus: Ohio State Univ. Press, 1974], 62). Because both Motley's romance and Hawthorne's sketch were first published in 1849, there is small likelihood of any literary influence.

of the Puritan was to evolve into the libertarian self-reliance of the Yankee revolutionary, Motley can admit the flaws in the Puritan temper, yet still condone its historical achievements. After portraying Endicott as a ranting bigot with a fast sword and a mouth full of dogma, Motley tells us "such a man of iron, rigid, incisive character was, perhaps, the true and only instrument by which the first foundations of the Puritan Commonwealth could have been hewn out in that stern and rocky wilderness" (II, 123).

Motley's determination to light "a spark of sympathy for the heroic souls of Puritan forefathers" could not be squared with his methods as historian and romancer. As a historian, Motley was sufficiently conscientious not to gloss over the severity of Morton's punishments; as a romancer, Motley had made Morton engaging by emphasizing the humor of Morton's book and the ironies of his life. Just as Adams was to feel obliged to condemn Morton after resurrecting him, so Motley can appreciate Morton's ingenuous gaiety because he believes Morton's ways should have been superseded in the march of progress. The difficulty of so compromised a judgment of Puritan virtue is that Motley arouses our respect for heroic Puritan souls only at the expense of our "sympathy" for them. When we are finally told why we must revere intolerant Puritan forefathers, for example, Motley must attempt to strike a precarious balance between justifying the arrival of a Christian civilization and simultaneously justifying the sheer force of America's manifest destiny: "It was a great movement, not a military, nor a philanthropic, nor a democratic movement, but a religious, perhaps a fanatical movement. Yet the movers were in earnest and the result was an empire" (II, 235). By means of such statements, restored facts are reinterpreted according to the values of 1849. After uncovering the mistreatment of Morton, Motley's commitment to the greater good of the westward course of empire has thus led him to rationalize it.

However one judges the timeliness of Motley's moralizing, *Merry Mount* nonetheless suggests the achievement of 19th century historical romance as history. A fiction, not a history, had first incorporated the *New English Canaan* into a historically defensible reconstruction of the Merry Mount controversy. Precisely because Motley wrote as a romancer rather than a regional historian, he was able to break through the encrusted prejudice and repeated phrases of New England historiography to allow Morton's viewpoint, legal and ethical, its first full hearing. Only after Motley had written his romance could he have confronted so somber and public a New England forum as the *North American Review* with a much exaggerated but necessary protest: "The Plymouth people were incensed beyond endurance at Morton's pranks and, squatters as they were themselves, could not refrain from inflicting lynch law upon a man whose only offense was dancing round a Maypole upon his own ground."[34]

* * *

William Carlos Williams' *In the American Grain* (1925) shares with Brooks' *America's Coming of Age* (1915), Bourne's "The Puritan's Will to Power" (1916), Mencken's "Puritanism as a Literary Force" (1917), and Lawrence's *Studies in Classic American Literature* (1923) a desire to trace the ills of modern America to the persistence of a bête noire called "Puritanism." Williams is frank in acknowledging his intent: "I wish to drag this THING out by itself to annihilate it. . . . There is a 'puritanism' of which you hear, of course, but you have never felt it stinking all about you—that has survived to us from the past. It is an atrocious thing, a kind of mermaid with a corpse for tail. Or it remains, a bad breath in the room."[35] *In The American Grain* ascribes to this Puritan legacy each of the national failings: will divorced from instinct, mind divorced from body, fear of touching, fear of nature, fear of sex, fear of minorities, xenophobia, obsessions with clean bodies and stored wealth, a repressed love of violence, an excessive regard for both civil law and abstract reasoning.

To summarize Williams' charges in this manner is to destroy the art with which he has selected passages, ordered historical events, and envisioned characters to render his viewpoint convincing. Historical figures whom Williams most admires—Red Eric, Montezuma, De Soto, Rasles, Boone, Burr—are iconoclasts who seek fulfillments beyond civilization and Christianity. They are men who in great measure have surrendered self to the senses or the wilderness, and have therefore been maligned or forgotten. The monologues or biographies which recreate them are imaginative history at its best: concrete in diction, intimate in tone, and free of deadening conventions of academic historiography. Those historical figures whom Williams least admires—Cortez, Bradford, Mather, Franklin, and Hamilton—are usually damned by quotations from their own writings, offered without comment but within an already existing scheme of values. As the essays build upon one another, the act of descending to one's origins repeatedly defines redemption. While explorers rediscover the Indian, pioneers rediscover the land, and poets rediscover their locality, Williams and his reader rediscover a historical heritage which subsumes all three. One insistent metaphor seems increasingly apt. The Puritan, spiritless

---

[34] Motley, "The Polity of the Puritans," *North American Review,* 69 (1849), 487.
[35] *In the American Grain* (New York: New Directions, 1956), 115.

inventor of his soul, resembles a hard little seed which, by refusing to risk rooting itself in the land, lost all prospect of blossoming.

To define the inner failure of the Puritan settlement, Williams selected an event readily adaptable to his values. His essay "The May-pole at Merry Mount" borrows all its material from Adams' edition of the *New English Canaan,* yet inverts Adams' conclusions. Because Morton never wronged the Indians, his trading of guns and liquor to them may have been unfair competition, but not moral error. Williams follows Hawthorne, not Adams, in insisting that Merry Mount was destroyed for its moral, rather than economic, offenses. The May Day revels, which show only Morton's sensual surrender to the new land, were the "direct cause" (79) of Morton's arrest and deportation. The liquor, Maypole, and atheism do not concern Williams, who finds that Puritan sexual attitudes were the source of controversy. The Puritans laid their hands "with malice, with envy, insanely" upon Morton, simply because he had laid hands upon that red flesh which they desired, yet feared to touch. Morton thus emerges, for the first time, as a natural man victimized by repressed authoritarians and a bad press.

The destruction of Merry Mount provided Williams with his example for the immediate triumph of those historical forces associated, no longer with progress to empire, but with spiritual and physical death. Unlike Motley, who had relished Morton's character while disapproving of it, Williams makes no attempt to vivify Morton, protagonist though he is. Here the difficulty lies in Williams' acute perception of Morton's "lightness, his essential character, which discloses the Puritans themselves as maimed, to their advantage, for survival" (76). It is true that Williams' Puritans subdue nature, win the continent, and maim their own spirits, precisely because of their deadening gravity. And yet, Williams' most admired men, those who most fully accept the wilderness, are certainly not light of spirit. Red Eric, De Soto, Rasles, and Boone have precious little sense of gaiety. All brood over the mysterious darkness of the savage continent, and all find regeneration by dying back into the wilderness. Morton may serve very well as a symbolic victim, or as a faint forerunner of Rasles or Boone, but Williams has read too much of Morton's relish for profit, survival, and witticism to allow Morton more than his five pages.

Williams' suggestion that Puritan hatred of Morton's community grew from repressed sexual envy became the central motif of Richard Stokes' *Merry Mount* (1932), a dramatic poem which, somewhat shortened, served as the libretto for Howard Hanson's opera one year later. The central figure and representative Puritan of both works is Wrestling Bradford, a self-conscious pietist tormented by his detested longing for "fair lascivious concubines of Hell/ With dewy flanks and honey scented breasts,/ Who tug away the covers, prick my flesh/ With hands of fire."[36] The Merry Mounters, led by good-natured Thomas Morton, Sir Gower Lackland, and Lady Marigold Sandys, are a "company of merry gentlemen," quite indifferent to money, politics, guns, or Indians, who seek only "an Empire of Jollity/ with song and pastime/ Revel and Maypole Dance" (65–66). Wrestling Bradford's instantaneous "lust" for Lady Marigold is perverted into sadistic violence when she asks Bradford to marry her to Sir Gower during the May Day ceremonies. After leveling the maypole and shooting Sir Gower, the Puritans drive the Indians to exact vengence through arson. Aroused by his fantasy that Lady Marigold is Ashtoreth, Wrestling Bradford signs the Devil's book in exchange for one night of carnal sin. Both poem and opera conclude with a lurid scene in which Bradford, maddened by "loathed ecstasy" (249), the devil's brand visible on his forehead, seizes Lady Marigold in his arms and strides into his burning City of God proclaiming "Beloved, beloved, come and drain with me the Wine of Death" (273).

The immediacy of Williams' historiography and the power of Hanson's music should not obscure the historical falsity of these reconstructions. By ascribing unfailing hysteria and hyperbole to Puritan speech, men are turned into monsters; the maypole becomes simply an object of apocalyptic rage fed by forbidden desires. Due to the total absence of evidence to substantiate these interpretations, one must conclude that Williams and Stokes were prepared to impose new values upon history.[37] Stokes' poem, indeed, reads like an unconscious parody of clichés about the 1920s: contempt for fathers, longing for frank sensuality, suspicion of all political behavior, and association of grace or art with Europe. Stokes and Williams suppose a Puritan absolutism in order to condemn it absolutely. To fix the devil's brand upon Wrestling Bradford is a judgment more "Puritan" in its severe, Manichean certainty than any judgment William Bradford would have been likely to risk.

By rescuing the controversy from the simplistic revisionism of Williams and Stokes, Stephen Vincent Benét faced, as Motley and Adams had done before him, the patriotic demand to disparage an engaging reprobate. In "The Devil and Daniel Webster," Benét selects Morton as one member of

[36] *Merry Mount*, music by Howard Hanson, libretto by Richard Stokes (New York: Harms, Inc., 1933), 40.

[37] By 1930 Samuel Eliot Morison was sufficiently weary of debunkers' distortions to protest "We have so often been told how Morton's downfall was due to the Pilgrims' hatred of mirth and jollity, that it is worth noting the facts" (*Builders of the Bay Colony* [Cambridge: Houghton Mifflin, 1930], 16).

the twelve-man devil's jury of American history; because of his "flushed, loose, handsome face and his hatred of the Godly," Morton is thus grouped with Simon Girty and Teach the Pirate.[38] *Western Star* (1943), Benét's uncompleted epic about the age of settlement, argues that the Puritans had to have "hated" Morton once they knew of the "stark matter of life and death" involved in trading guns to Indians.[39] On both occasions, however, Benét's reproval is softened because defeated opponents like Morton played essential roles in the triumph of Benét's underlying hero, the idea of American national union. The devil's jury is rightly persuaded by god-like Daniel to free Jabez Stone from the devil's clutches; all twelve are later forgiven because they "played a part in America" and thereby made "something new" (49). In *Western Star,* the Puritans' conquest of the continent allows Benét unreservedly to enjoy the exuberance of Morton's character: "The one man with a sense of humor in all New England"; "The last flare of Old England"; "He drank the country down like a cup of sack" (166). Because Thomas Morton "loved the country" (166), he thus seems, amid the heady patriotism of war years, to be a Falstaffian scamp whose faults were minor and English. No account of Morton before or after Benét's could afford to be so accepting of both historical opponents.

Robert Lowell's one-act play, *Endicott and the Red Cross* (1964), combines the May Day celebration of 1627, Endicott's expedition to cut down the Maypole in 1629, Winthrop's burning of Merry Mount in 1630, Gorges' scheme to take over New England, and Endicott's cutting the red cross from the British flag, all into the events of one day at Merry Mount in the 1630s. Hawthorne's Edith, Edgar, and Peter Palfrey reappear, and many phrases from Bradford, Morton, and Hawthorne are worked unobtrusively into the dialogue. Lowell's play shows a scrupulous regard, not for historical dates, but for the words of the written tradition which historians and novelists had created. Quotations and events are combined into a drama which, though free of antiquarianism, fundamentally alters that tradition. Lowell is not concerned to prove that the demise of Merry Mount represents historical progress or decline, nor to create exemplars of persecuted sensualists or worthy founders. Whereas Benét could refuse to condemn because the march of history was benign, Lowell will not choose, because his historical vision allows for little hope. Freedom of will and action, which had always been preserved for both parties, no longer exists. Whatever Puritans or Merry Mounters may profess, they are compelled by circumstances toward pragmatic decisions which only

---

[38] *The Devil and Daniel Webster* (New York: Farrar and Rinehart, 1937), 42.
[39] Benét, *Western Star* (New York: Farrar and Rinehart, 1943), 166.

work, in differing ways, to their self-destruction. Thus, Lowell's concern
is the muddle of motivation in historical event, the problems which that
muddle poses for statecraft, and the consequent sham of the nation's
old glory.

Lowell has freed Morton from previous, merely judgmental identities
as a devil, cavalier, joyous hedonist, or misunderstood Anglican. The
gaily dressed gentleman of Hawthorne, Motley, and Stokes appears on stage
"overweight" and dressed in a "shabby coffee-colored suit, part cloth and
part deerskin," a costume which suggests frontier exigencies, not English
origins.[40] Morton feels no yearning for "noblemen, cathedrals, or plays"
because he has established Merry Mount for three New World purposes:
"love" of the "rough land," "money," and "renewal" (11). Lowell's New
England, however, is neither Canaan nor a virgin but "a waste of animals,
Indians and the nine-month winter" (25). Moreover, Morton's small community is constantly threatened by clever royal agents, Puritan killers, and
savages who are savages. As the play develops, Morton's declared love of
land is replaced by disgust for Puritans and politicians; he says nothing of
the money he has made, nor of any regeneration.

The grimness of Morton's situation accounts for major changes in his
character. His powers of ridicule and irony are less a sign of boisterous
flippancy than a device for self-protection. The falconer who had quoted
Ovid, the sensualist who had sought the natural life, now is overheard
reducing the options and meanings of his world to joyless practicalities
expressed in flat diction and curt phrases. Of his society at Mount
Wollaston, Morton says "It's very lonely here" (17); of his trade, "We
have to give them liquor and guns to get their furs" (24); of kings and
churches, "Our supply of both is endless" (21); of his life in the New
World, "I have a plantation. I have to make it pay, I have to live" (17).
Because Morton's survival demands playing off Indians, Puritans, and the
home government against each other, he habitually dehumanizes his world
by metaphor. He calls his white followers "animals," the Indians "beasts,"
the Puritans "May-flies," then plans to divert Laud's soldiers with red concubines because "you've got to throw these dogs a little flesh/ if you want
them to fight the Puritans" (16).

Unlike any predecessor, Lowell sees Morton as a disillusioned pragmatist resorting to continual pretense simply in order to get by. The May
Day revels, for example, are a mask behind a mask, two contrasting and
successive ceremonies, both of them facades. To titillate and shock Black-

[40] Robert Lowell, *The Old Glory*, rev. ed. (New York: Farrar, Straus and Giroux,
1965), 9. These three plays include *Endicott and the Red Cross*.

stone, Morton arranges to read "doggerel . . . in a buffoonish singsong," while his revellers "dance obscenely" and show themselves to be "animals" (13–14). As soon as Blackstone objects to lewdness and threatens reprisal, Morton calls for "a stately and sedate dance," in which the same revellers are "ladies and gentlemen" pretending to be shepherds (15). When the perplexed Blackstone observes, "you are very changeable and double-faced here," Morton merely justifies his duplicity by saying "The world is changeable. It's like a playing card" (16). And yet, because Morton holds losing cards, his cynicisms end in willful displays of futility. When Morton returns on stage to witness the destruction of his community, we see him, for the first time in the written tradition, simply as a human being beaten and stripped of his defenses, "partly drunk, but more in a state of despairing recklessness" (55).

As a class, Lowell's Puritans offer even less promise for a nation than Morton. Simple-minded Peter Palfrey, the representative Puritan in the play, truly is, in Morton's phrase, "a Bible mangling donkey" (57). By dramatizing sadistic Puritan judgments mentioned in Hawthorne's stories, Lowell shows us ministers and militia brutalizing envied deviants in the name of God, much as Williams and Stokes had done. Writing in the 1960s, however, Lowell attributes greater importance to the implacable hostility between Puritans and Indians. Although the Puritans say they are leveling Merry Mount "to enforce moral decorum" (58), Lowell devises an incident to heighten the expedition's racial overtones. Having established a blood brotherhood with Sachem Assawamsett, Morton has traded to the Indians rifles they may have used to murder Judge Bowden, whose death the Puritans have come to Merry Mount to avenge.

In spite of Lowell's distaste for forefathers, however, he will not allow his Puritans to become the conveniently villainous scapegoats of the 1920s. The most perceptive and complex character in the play is the destroyer of Merry Mount, John Endicott. No longer Hawthorne's "Puritan of Puritans" (64), sure of his rectitude and proud of his severity, Endicott is the only figure in Lowell's play to recognize that "Each city is a Jerusalem" (45), "Nothing is clear" (44), "No one is too clean or free" (60). After butchering Assawamsett, shooting all of Morton's Indians, and burning Merry Mount to the ground, Endicott subverts his triumph by proclaiming "a day of mourning" both for himself and "for the other Indians, all those who are fighting/ with unequalled ferocity, and probably hopeless courage,/ because they prefer annihilation to the despair of our conquest" (77). It is John Endicott who, by insisting that all flags arouse destructively simplistic responses, introduces a truth crucial to all three plays in *The Old Glory.*

Endicott compels the audience to recognize the personal and political circumstances which have induced him to act as he does. He knows that his Puritan absolutism is a compensation for inner emptiness: "When my wife died, I served in the army./ Somehow I found I couldn't stomach killing/ without an iron faith. I found that iron faith" (42). His Calvinism is only a rationale for outbursts of military violence which provide him with momentary life at the expense of lingering guilt. When Palfrey expresses anxiety that the glorious New Israel may fall, Endicott grimly admits that he can sustain trust neither in Christianity nor in the future of Salem: "I have little faith. The faith of the armies./ I am only alive when I am fighting for my life./ I detest this, but it is so" (49).

Endicott's doubts lead him into ever swifter brutalities, followed by ever deepening depression. He enters acknowledging "I am the hollowness inside my armor" (41). Soon he dreams that he is a "Jesuit general . . . reading black sentences on the black page of a ribboned book," forever condemning a world of nameless men to death with the approval of his self-made God (45–47). Before cutting the red cross from the flag, Endicott declares, as in Hawthorne's tale, "What have we to do with England," but the lengthy speech that follows, one which Hawthorne had regarded as a glorious premonition of national independence, is to Lowell's Endicott merely rhetoric, "a hollow dishonest harangue,/ half truth, half bombast" (50). Whether Endicott uses guns or words, he knows he is only playing out cards dealt him in a historical game which no one fully understands. His ability to act decisively has made him Governor of Salem; as Governor of that frontier village he must crush all opposition, red or white. Early in the play, Endicott had tried futilely to explain New England statecraft to Palfrey:

> A statesman can either work with merciless efficiency
> and leave a desert;
> or he can work in a hit-and-miss fashion
> and leave a cesspool (48).

Although Lowell never suggests that a more human creed is practicable, he shows us the repulsive consequences of Endicott's expediency. Knowing that Assawamsett may not be responsible for Judge Bowden's murder, Endicott nonetheless orders the Sachem's body to be cut into one hundred pieces, then gives the dead hand to Thomas Morton.

The intent of Lowell's characterization of Endicott is elusive, but the analogies which suggest themselves are modern. Insofar as Endicott's outlook is dark, doubting, and fond of historical irony, he resembles Robert Lowell. The brutality and seeming assurance of Endicott's military decisions might have reminded certain viewers in a 1965 audience of Robert McNamara or Lyndon Johnson. Those who find comfort in ideological labels could arguably perceive Endicott as an Existentialist turned Fascist. Whomever Endicott might recall, however, he little resembles the forthright, pious Endicott of Mayo's biography. The self-conscious doubts and weary role playing in which Endicott, like Morton, is mired, are perfectly suited to the mood of *Götterdammerung* now surrounding the dawn of American civilization. At Merry Mount, on May Day, Robert Lowell's Queen of the May laments for "Eden gone before it began" (12).

*   *   *

Midway through a post-Civil War speech reassuring Americans and Englishmen that "our law is Progress, the result Democracy,"[41] Ambassador Motley acknowledged unexpected doubts about the worth of historical writing:

> There is no such thing as human history. We have a leaf or two, which we decipher as best we can, with purblind eyes, and endeavor to learn their mystery as we float along to the abyss; but it is all confused babble— hieroglyphics of which the key is lost (4).

Such a conclusion might be reached by anyone attempting to recover, through the primary sources about Merry Mount, a historical event of whole and consistent meaning. The very existence of Motley's romance, however, shows his eloquent statement to be needlessly gloomy. *Merry Mount* had restored historical leaves and provided a new key—without introducing confusion. In dismissing historiography as babble, Motley has momentarily forgotten that the entire literature of a past event can comprise a history of changing cultural fears and values. Most importantly, he has ignored the constructive value of his own historical disillusionment. In recreating Merry Mount, those writers most sure of the existence of a historical truth, or most determined to find a moral law operating in events, have been least attentive to the implications of the extant historical record. Those who have admitted to conflicting values and the partiality of evidence have been freed to create suggestive possibilities from the shards which remain. When similar distortions of character appear in Stokes' libretto and Slotkin's history, whereas plausible reconstructions appear in Motley's romance and Lowell's play, distinctions of genre and profession based upon notions of history and non-history lose their utility.

---

[41] Motley, *Democracy: The Climax of Political Progress and the Destiny of Advanced Races* (London: n.p., 1869), 6.

IN SEARCH OF
"THE SPIRIT OF '76"

THOMAS H. PAULY
University of Delaware

BY THE END OF THE BICENTENNIAL CELEBRATION EVERY AMERICAN CITIZEN
will undoubtedly recognize "The Spirit of '76." All year long its three tat-
tered, patriotic musicians have been doing a heroic job reminding us of our
Revolution and the most essential products of our modern culture. They
have been pictured leading the way for such diverse organizations as Budget
Rent-A-Car, the American Chiropractic Association, and Sesame Street.
The English even recruited them to promote British Airways. This painting
has been used in so many adaptations that its title is recalled with difficulty,
and only devotees of historical trivia can name the man who actually painted
it. Like the dying foreground figure who is usually cropped out (e.g. the com-
memorative stamp issued by the Postal Service), Archibald Willard has
been left by the wayside, unable to share in the triumph of the valiant trio he
created (see Plate 1).

Information on the forgotten painter of this hallmark of American
popular culture is scarce and highly inaccurate. *The Spirit of '76* by Henry
Kelsey Devereux, who posed for the drummer boy, is the main source, but
the twelve pages devoted to Willard are filled with distortions and errors.
Moreover his account was published in 1928 in a private printing of only 500
copies. Anne Colver, Willard's great-niece, has written a second book
entitled *Yankee Doodle Painter,* but it is essentially a children's book about
"Uncle Arch." The few articles on Willard and his painting do little more

*Picture Credits (Clockwise from upper right hand corner): *The New Yorker* (artist: W. Cotton); *Our Daily Bread* (United Artists); *Budget Rent-A-Car; Saratoga* Cigarettes (Phillip-Mor-
ris); *Sesame Street Calendar* (artist: Michael J. Smollin); Dustcover, *Americana in Miniature*
by Estelle Ainsley Worrell (Van Nostrand Reinhold); U.S. Postal Service Bicentennial Com-
memorative Stamp; *New York Times; Sheraton Inns; American Chiropractic Assn.; Children's
Library Poster; Corporate Report* (artist: Bob Pasciunas); *Esquire* (artist: Burt Silverman);
Borden Inc.; Kentucky Fried Chicken; New York Times. Center: "Yankee Doodle"—original
chromolithograph (Library of Congress).

than echo Devereux.[1] No less frustrating than the anecdotal character of these accounts is their assumption that readers would want to know about only the forty years of Willard's life that led up to his great work; of the remaining forty-two not a word has been printed.

An equal amount of mystery surrounds the painting itself. The original is generally presumed to be hanging in Abbot Hall in Marblehead, Massachusetts, but there are "Spirits of '76" in the Western Reserve Historical Society in Cleveland and in a private gallery in New York which have each staked published claims to being *the* original.[2] And these are not all; there are approximately fifteen such "Spirits." Though most of these have been quite reticent about their date of birth, all are believed to have come from the hand of the master—and probably did. Ironically, should any one of these ever be able to prove that it is indeed *the* original, it would have to abdicate its renowned title and become "Yankee Doodle," since this was the name under which it was first exhibited at the Philadelphia Centennial Exhibition of 1876. Only after the Exhibition did it acquire the name by which it is currently known.

At the center of all this confusion lurk two very puzzling questions. How could the creator of such a widely recognized piece have remained so obscure? Moreover, how did this one work by such an unknown ever emerge from an exhibition of thousands of paintings, literally acres of them, and go on to become one of the most famous creations of any American painter? My search for satisfactory answers to these questions involved retracing the footsteps of a man whose work sprang from his own return to the events of a hundred years earlier. In addition to visiting the original Centennial Exhibition, I found myself detoured into the early development of photography and encountered one of its pioneers, James F. Ryder, who was as resourceful a businessman as he was accomplished with his Voightlander lens. If the vain efforts of the painter to rise again to the one great achievement of his limited talent even more closely align him with the fallen figure in the foreground, Ryder might be associated with the triumphant musicians, for it was the enterprising determination of his promotion that put them on the road to fame.

* * *

What is known of Willard's early life consists of a bare handful of facts so embellished with latter-day recollections and local myth-making that it

[1]Anne Colver, *Yankee Doodle Painter* (New York: Knopf, 1955); Alberta Thorne Daywalt, "The Spirit of '76," *Antiques,* 40 (July 1911), 24; "The Spirit of '76," *American Heritage,* 12 (Aug. 1961), 57. Devereux's book, it is worth noting, relies heavily on an earlier article by James F. Ryder, "The Painter of 'Yankee Doodle'," *New England Magazine,* 13 (Dec. 1895), 483–94.

[2]Daywalt, 24. See also Elbert J. Benton, *Cultural Story of An American City* (Cleveland: Western Reserve Historical Soc., 1943), III, 80–83; *Art in America,* 61 (July 1973), 12.

Plate 1: "The Spirit of '76" and Variations*

reads like Parson Weems' folktale *Life of George Washington*. Willard was
born in Bedford, Ohio, and for the first seventeen years of his life led a
transient existence in the company of his father, who was an itinerant
Baptist minister. Long before graffiti came to be seen as the forceful
expression of the untrained, unrecognized artist, he is said to have spread his
"humorous scrawls on barn doors, board fences, and every smooth surface
available."[3] He then settled in Wellington and went to work as a painter for
a local wagon maker, E. S. Tripp. Though he began in a broad-brush position, he was soon doing the elaborate ornamentation and calligraphy commonly applied to wagons of this era.

During the Civil War Willard served in the 86th Ohio Regiment, but he
saw little action and was soon back at his former job. As an idle diversion
some years later he painted for Tripp's daughter, Addie, a pair of pictures
featuring a cart of children being pulled by a dog in pursuit of a rabbit (see
Plates 2 and 3). In the first, entitled "Pluck," three children are depicted as
tumbling about and spilling over the side amidst the frenzy of the chase. In
"Pluck" No. 2, the dog has caught his prey but the cart has been shattered
against a log and the children lie draped amidst the wreckage. The pictures,
we are told, were taken to be framed by a Cleveland photographer, James F.
Ryder, who found they attracted such attention he had them turned into
chromolithographs, a currently popular process for making color prints.[4]
Willard's humorous tale of the smashed cart proved so successful it ended
his association with Tripp. He moved to Cleveland where, after some additional training in New York, he completed his "Yankee Doodle." The standard explanation of how this piece came to be included in the Centennial
Exhibition in Philadelphia usually rounds out the hagiography of Willard, the
people's painter. First circulated as chromos in the streets about Fairmount
Park, the subject generated so much interest that Willard was extended a
belated invitation to put his painting on display in one of the prominent
galleries.[5] One account relates how Willard subsequently received his
supreme accolade late one night in the main hall while he was repairing a
tear in his canvas caused by the pressing crowd of viewers. On a tour of the
closed buildings, President Grant pauses before the painting and tells the
officer accompanying him, "Good . . . Tell Mr. Willard I think his picture is
good."[6] Like the fairy tale angel of good tidings, he then fades into the night.

This scene of the General-turned-President stopping to pay respect to the
inspiring battle scene depicted by another Civil War veteran is touching, but,

[3]Daywalt, 24.
[4]James F. Ryder, *Voightlander and I: In Pursuit of Shadow Catching* (Cleveland: Cleveland
Printing Co., 1902), 216; see also Henry Kelsey Devereux, *"The Spirit of '76": Some Recollections of the Artist and the Painting* (Cleveland: Arthur H. Clark Co., 1926), 29.
[5]Devereux, 30–31, 67; *American Heritage,* 57; Daywalt, 24.
[6]Colver, 167.

Plate 2

like most of what has been reported about Willard's involvement with the Exhibition, it is pure fiction. Grant only visited the Exhibition for the opening and closing ceremonies, and they would have been most unlikely times for Willard to have been repairing his canvas. Also "Yankee Doodle" did not hang in the Main Building, which featured general interest displays and involved few paintings. It wasn't even on display in Memorial Hall, the gigantic building exclusively intended for art exhibits. Finally "Yankee Doodle" was not included in the Exhibition either by popular demand or after its opening. During the show's six-month run from May 10 to November 10, the official catalogue passed through seven different editions and, through all of them, either as item No. 468 or 866, "Yankee Doodle" continued to hang in gallery No. 10 of the Art Annex. Willard's original application for exhibition space was made seven months before the fair opened and, at that time, the director of the art exhibits, John Sartain, was so distressed by the flood of applications he quickly mounted plans for an additional building. Consequently any delay that may have occurred in assigning Willard's painting a place is probably best explained by the confusion prevailing during the months immediately following his application.

The most important point of misunderstanding, however, is the enormous

Plate 3

popularity the painting is believed to have enjoyed. The claim of a flier distributed at Abbot Hall that the painting "stirred the heart of the nation" is
simply not true. Approximately a hundred guides to the Exhibition were
published for visitors, but "Yankee Doodle" is noted in only a couple and, as
one might expect, they were the ones which specialized in elaborate coverage
of the art exhibition. The same holds for newspaper accounts. Since only
experienced critics would have attempted any extensive discussion of the
art, the evaluation of this commentator appears hardly surprising: "There is
a great waste of good material here, and Mr. Willard's work is rather op-
pressive."[7] Although this criticism was counterbalanced by praise for the
work's "inspiration," these remarks turn out to have been unique simply because their author ventured a judgment. In all the other cases where the
painting was mentioned, it was only identified or there was a brief comment
on its widespread fame as a print. "Willard's 'Yankee Doodle', so well
known by its countless reproductions, occupies a good half of the northern
wall," noted one,[8] while another echoed, "Willard's now celebrated picture

---

[7]Quote found in an unidentified collection of newspaper clippings held by the Historical Society of Pennsylvania (H.S.P.).
   [8]Undated clipping in scrapbooks (H.S.P.).

entitled 'Yankee Doodle' is known by the lithographs and engravings, and
will be welcome here in the original."[9] In other words, even at its initial
showing Willard's painting attracted attention only because it had already
been seen elsewhere.

While it is commonly known that Willard's picture was widely circulated
as a print, this point has never been accorded the importance it merits.
However much "Yankee Doodle" may have engaged the taste of the
populace, it could never have gained widespread recognition without some
very effective form of mass distribution. Without a concrete reminder to jog
the memory, the most impressive sights are often soon forgotten. This is
especially true of a gigantic exhibition where thousands of unique items
compete to gain the eye's attention. Moreover, to have become as well
known as this picture did it had to be seen by people who never could have
had contact with the actual painting. Only prints would explain the strange
turn of affairs whereby Conrad's "The American Soldier," Maynard's
"1776," Guarnerio's statue of "Washington," and the group sculpture
entitled "America" drew both the crowds and the critics' attention, while
the frequently bypassed "Yankee Doodle" in the Annex went on to become
famous.

All the interest generated by the Centennial Exhibition along with the
diversified crowd of visitors provided an ideal environment in which to launch
a rise to fame, but the most essential factor in doing so was to understand
this situation and to capitalize on its potential. No man was better prepared
or in a better position to do this than James F. Ryder. As essential as he was
to the success of "Yankee Doodle," Ryder also provides the most reliable
source of information about Willard. Quite simply, Ryder was an indus-
trious, outgoing man of affairs. Besides his autobiography, *Voightlander and
I: In Pursuit of Shadow Catching,* he, unlike Willard, left behind a trail of
correspondence and numerous retrievable records of his activities which
make it possible to trace just how "The Spirit of '76" was able to march over
all its competition (see Plates 4 and 5).

Ryder came to Ohio from his native New York as a somewhat itinerant
daguerrotypist. His experience quickly taught him that the man who could
create the most attractive image had the most customers and so he always
made it a practice to keep abreast of all the current developments in his
field. Once he established himself in Cleveland, he began making periodic
trips to study the new merchandise in New York photographic shops. He
closely followed the various trade journals as they came into existence. By
the late 1860s he evolved a specialized interest in retouching negatives and

[9] Frank H. Norton, *Illustrated Historical Register of the Centennial Exposition, 1876* (New
York: American News Co., 1878), 202. See also R. S. Fletcher, *Art Glances: A Companion to
the Art Gallery* (Philadelphia: S. T. Souder, 1876), 89.

Plate 4: James F. Ryder.   Plate 5: Archibald M. Willard.

tinting them with water colors and India ink. Just as he had once commissioned an authority on the new process of ambrotinting, at $100 a class,
to share his knowledge,[10] so he now paid the travel expenses of a German
expert in order to gain expertise in retouching photos.[11]

About the same time, he learned that some of his fellow photographers
were eager to start a National Photographic Union in order to promote the
developing concerns of the profession. Though this was essentially a
Philadelphia-based organization spearheaded by Edward L. Wilson to defeat
a stranglehold patent on cutting bromide, Ryder lent his support quickly and
enthusiastically. First he organized a subsidiary Northern Ohio
Photographic Society and then served on the original executive committee at
the first national convention in 1869. The force of his influence brought the
second convention to Cleveland, where its several thousand members
gathered to celebrate its successful defeat of the bromide patent.

This ready willingness to invest in anyone or any undertaking that might
profit him professionally is essential to understanding Ryder's association
with Willard. Up to the end of World War II, there were few photography
studios that were able to survive on their camera work alone. Usually they
offered framing materials, a variety of printed illustrations, often books, and
sometimes even curios. Despite all his intense concern for the technical and
organizational development of his profession, Ryder was no less vigilant re-

[10] *Voightlander and I,* 125.
[11] In a review of a book on painting photographs, *The Philadelphia Photographer* [6 (Nov.
1869), 1] announced: "Mr. Ryder of Cleveland, Ohio, has gone so far in this matter to import an
artist for this special work, from Germany, and found it a profitable investment."

garding the commercial importance of these related services. In 1872, when he moved to a larger studio and better location, Ryder began offering his customers more than a thousand fine English and French engravings from which to choose.[12] The elitist appeal of this initial offering quickly underwent sharp modification for, within months, Ryder was explaining to readers of the Cleveland *Leader:* "When the common intellect became elevated, the genius of art sank down a step to meet it, and spreading out in steel engravings, photographs and chromos, gave every one the means to adorn the most humble home." In support of this rationale, he announced that the popular Prang chromolithographs had been added to his selection along with "superb mottoes that will adorn a wall and make a home cheerful."[13]

Such was the chain of developments that led to "Pluck" 1 and 2. For these Ryder himself served as publisher and thereby added yet another dimension to his expanding list of involvements. According to Ryder, the exhibited paintings occasioned so many inquiries that he called upon the H. T. Anthony Company in New York to see if they would be interested in bringing out the pair as chromolithographs. When he was told that the only market lay in "illuminated mottoes representing Scriptural subjects and texts, as 'God bless our home,' etc.," he so doubted this advice that he decided to strike out on his own.[14]

Since this undertaking would have had little support for its prospects and involved a considerable financial risk, it seems most unlikely that Ryder would have acted quite so impulsively. In fact the alliance between Ryder and Willard on this venture was the product of much more extensive dealings. In his personal correspondence, Ryder acknowledged that his acquaintance with Willard extended as far back as 1862, when he photographed and sold sketches drawn by Willard.[15] Never mentioned, even in his letters, is the collection of Willard's work Ryder copyrighted in the early 1870s and sold in the form of cabinet photographs. These pieces, which carry titles such as "A Stitch in Time Saves Nine," "An Ounce of Prevention is Worth a Pound of Cure," "Contentment is Better than Riches," are "mottoes," probably the ones referred to in his advertisement. In contrast to those Ryder associated with the Anthony Company, these are all humorous, the situation in the picture undercutting the pretentious wisdom of the epigram. In other words, Ryder had already established that the glut of sentimental mottoes had created a strong market for the humor of his "Plucks."

Given this different set of facts, the placement of the two paintings in his

[12]Cleveland *Leader* (Sept. 9, 1872), 4.
[13]*Leader* (Feb. 1, 1873), 4.
[14]*Voightlander and I*, 218.
[15]Letter dated July 23, 1895, held by the Herrick Memorial Library (H.M.L.) in Wellington, Ohio.

show window was calculated advertisement rather than a coincidental display. Moreover, it exemplifies the care and shrewdness with which Ryder approached this undertaking. Since H. T. Anthony was principally a distributor of photographic supplies, Ryder's inquiry—whether it actually took place or not—indicates the importance these firms had as clearinghouses for all sorts of engravings and sheds light on the extent to which Ryder's venture represented an attempt to go into competition with them. In addition to the illustrated ads which were run continuously for three months in Cleveland newspapers and appeared in papers as far away as South Bend, Indiana, Ryder made a concerted effort to persuade his fellow photographers to use their studios as retail outlets. Taking full advantage of the influence he now wielded within the National Photographic Union, he secured special coverage for his undertaking from all the trade journals. Thus a front-page column of *The Photographic Times* announced: "Ha! ha! Our friend Ryder is certainly *out in new* colors to say the least . . . Every photographer in the land can sell dozens of copies (Mr. Ryder offers special terms to the trade), and before Christmas time the whole country will be screaming over this double demonstration of that plentious element in the American baby—young and old—pluck! No doubt Mr. Ryder will be well repaid for the pluck *he* evinces in undertaking the introduction of these pictures."[16] *The Philadelphia Photographer* announced these new chromos and posed the question, "What shall we say about them?" The glowing praise which followed concluded, "The entire scene is so full of spirit and life and so natural that every one must buy the pair. They should by all means be hung in every photographic reception room, in order to put your sitters in good humor. They teach a moral lesson also, i.e. he who pluckily holds on, wins."[17] These recommendations certainly must have increased sales for Ryder, but one cannot read these without sensing the barbed edge to their jocular tone. Both editors intimate that his merry pictures involved a little too much kitsch and putsch for their taste.

Little did they know just how enterprising the "plucky" Ryder really was. He arranged to have his chromos printed by the firm of Clay, Cosack and Company in Buffalo, New York. He probably made contact with this firm while attending the national convention of the Photographic Union held there during the summer of 1873 (the two "Plucks" came out late that fall—just in time for Christmas).[18] Ryder may not have fully comprehended the era's phenomenal interest in children as evidenced by the popularity of Frank Leslie's books, Horatio Alger's novels, *Little Women,* and *Tom Sawyer* (two years later), but he most definitely knew people were willing,

[16] *The Photographic Times,* 3 (Dec. 1873), 177–78.
[17] *The Philadelphia Photographer,* 10 (Dec. 1873), 580.
[18] *The Philadelphia Photographer,* 10 (Oct. 1873), 259.

even eager, to pay from $5 to $25 for a Prang chromo.[19] Consequently when he learned that Clay, Cosack would produce chromos of his pictures for 17 cents a piece,[20] he must have seen himself facing a rare opportunity. This price probably included additional expenses for printing preparations, promotion, and distribution, but the several thousand he sold at $10 a pair surely yielded a handsome profit. Immediately he persuaded Willard to establish a residence in Cleveland. When he next painted a picture of family prayers interrupted by a cat which has leaped upon the kneeling father's back, Ryder commissioned a supplementary poem from Bret Harte entitled "Deacon Jones' Experience" and brought out the combination in a chromo that was only slightly less successful than his first venture. Whatever his fellow photographers may have felt about Ryder's departure into chromos, they could not dispute the popularity of his offerings with their customers.

By the end of 1874 Ryder was already looking forward to the upcoming Centennial. From his Philadelphia colleagues, he learned of plans for a Photographers' Hall. On March 22, 1875, more than a year in advance of the Exhibition's opening and well before there was any assurance that the hall would actually be built, he filed a revealing application for exhibition. After describing his plans for a booth with pilasters, cornices, and a fifteen-foot counter, he announced "I am [a] manufacturer and dealer in photography and desire to sell my productions during the time of the Exhibition."[21] By way of preparation Ryder directed Willard to draft a series of pictures that would take advantage of the interest the Centennial was sure to generate. At this time both were thinking of something along the lines of their previous successes. Again they thought of pairing cartoon-like scenes which would be humorously associated with a famous motto or caption. One product, for example, was a barnyard scene of two chicks warring over a worm, entitled "United We Stand." In "Divided We Fall," the worm breaks and the chicks are sent tumbling. In the first of another pair, a boy associated with an eagle confronts another associated with a lion. Antagonism is reflected in the demeanor and countenance of all four. If the obtuse symbolism failed to impress its depiction of the spirit of the Revolution upon the viewer, the title drove the point home—"When in the course of human events, it becomes necessary." The second picture shows the lion and eagle hitched to a wagon and sleeping contentedly. While Uncle Sam reaches out to shake the hand of

---

[19]Larry Freeman, *Louis Prang: Color Lithographer* (Watkins Glen, N.Y.: Century House, 1971), 51–56.

[20]Walden Fawcett, "Story of Two Famous Pictures by Willard." Unidentified newspaper clipping in the Barton collection of information on Willard (H.M.L.). Internal evidence suggests that Ryder was the source of much of the information.

[21]Ryder's application (No. 2442), which is held in the Philadelphia City Archives, was among the first dozen for the Photographic Exhibition to be received. Since sales within the fairgrounds were strictly controlled, Ryder's plans had to be modified, but in a letter dated Feb. 23, 1876 (H.S.P.) Sartain gave Ryder special permission to include lithographs in his exhibit.

an approaching young man, he exclaims, "Why bless my heart, Johnny, you're welcome. How's your mother?" Apparently John Bull has come from Victorian England to visit the "Centennial Inn" pictured in the background (see Plates 6 and 7).

What makes these rather insipid creations interesting is the way Willard's patriotism undermines his humor. In the first picture the lion and eagle are too ferocious to be either comical or engaging. Moreover, the contrast between the two youths is weighted much too heavily to one side. The one associated with the eagle is a lean, stalwart lad of the Revolution whose loose workingman's attire accentuates his stance of fierce determination. Curiously the boy beside the lion is almost ten years younger. Wild-eyed and much too fat for his waistcoat and breeches, he is manifestly a spoiled cry-baby. Though the reconciliation of the second picture reduces this disparity, Uncle Sam remains the elder, the one who dominates the scene. John Bull has slimmed down (perhaps because he has divested himself of his colonies), but he is just now about the age of the young patriot in the first picture.

This tension helps to explain Willard's radical alteration of "The Spirit of '76" during the course of its creation. As originally conceived, "Yankee Doodle" was to be another piece of humor. Rather than the beleaguered, fighting yeomen of the Continental Army, his picture was to portray a merry band of musicians at a Fourth of July parade. In later years Willard even drafted a rude sketch illustrating these early intentions.[22] The evaporation of this projected humor is usually attributed to the growing illness of his father, who was posing for the central figure.[23] While there can be no doubt that the central figure is modeled upon Willard's father, the way he entered the picture and the effect he had on it was much more complex, since Rev. Samuel Willard died in 1874,[24] well before Willard began working on "Yankee Doodle."

Willard's closeness to his family had a very direct bearing on his art. Several of the earliest surviving examples of his work are portraits of family members or close friends. Though he abandoned this primitive style by 1870, he continued to paint his family and even used them as models in his other work. As an extension of this practice perhaps, Willard developed a strong interest in portraiture and, following the success of the two "Plucks," he traveled to New York to study under a specialist in this area, Joseph Oriel Eaton. The few weeks he worked with Eaton did little more than intensify his

[22]There is a picture of this sketch in Devereux's book.

[23]A flier distributed at Abbot Hall proclaims, "When the artist had sketched this picture, he looked about for living faces to represent his characters, for he knew that no imaginary picture could be more real than real life. In his father he found a face that suited him for a drummer." Ryder's article on Willard was the first to promulgate the story that Rev. Willard actually posed for his son and it has been repeated in every account since.

[24]A copy of the legal distribution of Willard's estate which gives his death date as 1874 is held by the Western Reserve Historical Society.

"When, in the course of human events it becomes necessary—"

Plate 6

Why bless my heart Johnny, you're Welcome! How's your mother?

Plate 7

Henry Devereux   Rev. Samuel Willard   Hugh Mosher

Plate 8

artistic aspirations, but by the middle of 1874, Willard had acquired enough skill that the Cleveland *Leader* was paid to announce that "in the production of oil portraits, the Ryders have secured the services of Mr. Willard."[25] Obviously Ryder was after the commercial benefits which might be derived from a truce to the heated war between photography and painting. Less obvious was the impact of this alliance upon Willard. In working with a photographer, he soon began working from photographs.

Willard's original idea for "Yankee Doodle" was inspired by the virtuosity of a drummer he had once seen and the accomplished fifing of his friend Hugh Mosher. Willard launched his project by having Mosher come and play for him, but a local photographer, William F. Sawtelle, was soon called in to take some photographs. Though he produced some fine pictures, Ryder was summoned to take more. Similarly, Willard's decision to insert his father as his central drummer might be traced to the impressive photograph Ryder had taken of the Rev. Willard just before he died. Finally, Ryder was called upon to photograph the young cadet Henry Devereux, whose association with the other two men gave the trio its striking character of embodying three generations (see Plate 8).

Though Willard and Ryder probably thought of these photographs as a mere convenience, they profoundly affected Willard's work. The faces of the three patriots in the painting bear such a strong resemblance to existing photographs that it is safe to conclude that Willard relied on the camera to give shape to his conception. Looking at the photograph of his stern evangelical father, he may well have reflected on the struggles of his father's life and recalled with pride the contribution his grandfather had made during the Revolution when he had fought with the Green Mountain Boys. To a man

[25] *Leader* (Feb. 12, 1874), 7.

with patriotic and familial feelings as strong as Willard's, this photograph of his recently deceased father was charged with meaning. It was also charged with a realism that was antagonistic to the technique of caricature he had used in his previous lithographic work. Thus Willard found himself at odds with his original intent of humor in his approach as much as in his emotional response to his material. At the same time one has only to look at the anachronistic flag in the background of his painting to know that Willard was no realist. Although Willard duplicated many of the elements of the photos he used, the effect of caricature is still quite evident. The face of the central figure, for example, is distorted so that it takes on a haggard determination while the fifer's has a bemused apish look that is almost comical—the contrast being one of the main sources of the picture's appeal. In short, the dramatic effect of the picture derived from more than the sentimental side of Willard's character.

By October of 1875, the work had been drafted, and Ryder knew that he had a winner. Quickly he wrote to have the picture copyrighted and began arranging to have it made into a chromo. Knowing how much the exhibition of the two "Plucks" had augmented sales, he himself filled out and mailed Willard's application for exhibition.[26] Willard was then put to work on an 8' × 10' version.

With calculated flair, Ryder launched his campaign. Throughout the first month of the Centennial year, he came out with front-page ads in the *Plain Dealer* and the *Leader* voicing his confidence that "a good sun will rise, HIGH IN THE HEAVENS, clear away the hanging mist, and give a golden tinge of restored prosperity to all." "With an abiding faith in YANKEE DOODLE and a belief that AMERICA IS A SUCCESS," he concluded with a wish that all his readers have a happy new year.[27] By March, the first chromos were run off. The opening of the Exhibition in May was attended with widespread advertisements in local newspapers, and again Ryder saw to it that the various trade journals came out with plugs for his offering.

For many, the conditions of the Exhibition were a source of confusion, but not for Ryder. In the first place, the most influential leaders of the Photographic Union resided in Philadelphia, and with them he had a long-standing friendship. Their studios provided him with valuable local outlets. Since the national convention of the Union was held in Philadelphia that year, these contacts would have also enabled him to take full advantage of this opportunity to acquaint his fellow photographers with his offering. Because this meeting took place that summer, several months after the Exhibition had been open, Ryder would have had the additional benefit of being

---

[26]Ryder's application for copyright was entered Oct. 27, 1875 (No. 11242). Willard's application for exhibition space was dated Oct. 23, 1875.

[27]*Plain Dealer* (Jan. 1, 1876), 1.

able to approach them with a product of proven marketability. In this respect, Ryder incurred an unexpected windfall in the rather peculiar pattern of the Exhibition's attendance. The first months saw the lowest attendance and the last months the highest, with steady growth in between. June, for example, averaged about 25,000 visitors a day while October attendance ran about 90,000, with more than 100,000 going each day in November.[28] Consequently the growing fame of the chromo would have had its impact on ever-increasing numbers of potential buyers.

Meanwhile additional benefits accrued from Ryder's continued association with Clay, Cosack and Company. By the middle seventies the firm had expanded sufficiently to have distributors in most of the country's major cities. This network undoubtedly aided the firm in its successful procurement of exclusive rights for all lithographic reproductions of the art exhibited at the Centennial Exhibition, though the contract was probably more a result of Ryder's connections, since Ryder's friends controlled the Centennial Photographic Co. which had exclusive rights to all photographs. In other words, "Yankee Doodle" was printed by the same house that was supplying an interested public with illustrations of the Exhibition's most famous attractions.

Most important of all, however, was Ryder's approach to pricing. The five dollars he had charged for each one of the previous chromos was dropped to three for an 18″ × 24″ print of "Yankee Doodle" so that, from the Exhibition's opening, he was offering not just a very attractive picture in one of the most popular processes of reproduction—but also one of the least expensive. Since Ryder also realized that the appeal of his product was closely tied with the atmosphere of the Centennial, he began discounting his stock as the Convention progressed. Amidst his mounting sales, Ryder held out his best deal to his fellow photographers. A full-page illustration in the November issue of *The Philadelphia Photographer* advertised "Yankee Doodle" for two dollars "with large discounts made to photographers and dealers." By now the picture was being offered by one of the nation's largest distributors of photographic supplies. By early 1877 the base price was dropped another fifty cents. No wonder years later the author of an article on the 1893 Chicago Exhibition in "The Illustrated World's Fair" would recall the powerful impression "Yankee Doodle" made upon him and note "the picture has become familiar in America, for copies and chromos of it may be seen in almost every public studio."[29]

There was an interesting irony in all these developments. Though it is little

[28] James D. McCabe, *The Illustrated History of the Centennial Exhibition* (Philadelphia: National Publishing Co., 1876), 845.

[29] Lyman J. Gage, "The World's Fair Celebrates Two Conquests," *The Illustrated World's Fair* (Aug. 1892), 282.

known, "Yankee Doodle" actually won an award, but not as a painting. Nor did it go to the painter. Rather it went to a photo of "Yankee Doodle" which Ryder had included in his display[30] and was presented with a special citation for the "skillful crayon work."[31] This honor acknowledged Ryder's studiously acquired expertise in painting photos, but it would probably have been more fitting if it had been for his skill in advertising and promotion since both this photo and his exhibit, which included Willard's other Centennial lithographs, were all part of his elaborate campaign to increase sales of the chromo.[32] Ryder, of course, never could have sold the public something it didn't want, but he certainly did everything he could to assure that the picture's potential would be fully realized. Like his marriage of Willard's painting and Harte's poem, Ryder's award-winning photo of "Yankee Doodle" would make a nice complement to the sentences which open the chapter "Luck and Work" in his autobiography: "In his march through life [a man] . . . must not be jostled or elbowed from the straight course. He can not halt and hold his place; the man behind would step in front of him."[33]

* * *

For a fragile moment, Willard stood before the open door of opportunity. Ryder's exploitation of the rapid methods of reproducing pictures demonstrated both the enormous market for these products and how inexpensively they might be made. Yet the future for the artist lay not in the sale of individual items, as Ryder had done so successfully, but rather in the field of illustration—pictures complementing the text of books and magazines. It was during the years immediately following the Centennial that Howard Pyle came to understand the implications of this revolution. He familiarized himself with the advantages and disadvantages of this developing technology and strove to adapt his talents to its new demands.[34] The title of the book containing some of Pyle's most successful early work, *Yankee Doodle* (1881), almost seems a backhanded compliment to the artist who had so successfully tapped the emerging tastes of a new audience. He pioneered what became a golden age of illustrators—N. C. Wyeth, Maxfield Parrish, Frederic Remington, Charles Dana Gibson, James Montgomery Flagg, and Norman Rockwell, who employed many of the same stylistic ele-

[30]Samuel J. Burr, *Memorial of the International Exhibition* (Hartford Conn.: L. Stebbins, 1877), 640.

[31]U.S. Centennial Commission, *Reports and Awards,* Francis A. Walker, ed. (Washington, D.C.: Government Printing Office, 1880), 7 (section 27), 682, #289.

[32]A description of the materials Ryder included in his exhibit can be found in *The Philadelphia Photographer,* 13 (June 1876), 198.

[33]*Voightlander and I,* 236.

[34]See Estelle Jussim, *Visual Communication and the Visual Arts* (New York: R. R. Bowker, 1974), 105–11.

ments to be found in Willard's pieces—yet they fully understood their medium, their audience, and their function as Willard never did. While publishers were not favorably disposed to the folksy humor toward which Willard naturally gravitated, his future career was hampered most by its very success. Blind to the function and impact of his chromos, he came to believe that he was a real artist in the traditional sense, the high priest with his oils.

Willard's major projects following the Centennial Exhibition assume the character of mad parodies of his achievement. First, he painted a picture variously entitled "The Divine Origin of the Flag," or "Stars and Stripes and the Magi" or more simply "Allegory of the Flag." First conceived as a small work and subsequently redone in mammoth dimensions just as he had done with "Yankee Doodle," this work was commissioned by Charles E. Latimer, the president of the Anti-Metric Society, who believed that the Anglo-American system of weights and measures had been divinely ordained. He urged Willard to shape his picture so that it depicted the progress of civilization toward personal freedom culminating in the achievement of America. A decade later he was again commissioned to do a set of murals for the courthouse in the town named Washington Court House, Ohio. These consisted of three large angels representing "The Spirit of Electricity," "The Spirit of the U. S. Mail," and "The Spirit of the Telegraph." In later years he again and again returned to the glorious American past, where he had won his fame, with paintings of "The Minute Men of the Revolution," "The Battle of Concord Hill," and a delightful "What Columbus Found" (Indians playing baseball) that was probably prepared to take advantage of the Columbian theme of the Chicago World's Fair.

For these as well as for his somewhat more accomplished efforts, there was not enough of a market to provide Willard with sufficient income on which to live. Wealthy Clevelanders in search of art looked to the Eastern cultural centers and Europe for their needs. Thus, in contrast to Ryder who continued to attract numerous customers for his photography and inexpensive art work, Willard found it increasingly difficult to make ends meet. During the years immediately following the Exhibition, he sold several paintings and did more humorous lithographs for Ryder, but his living came largely from the royalties of the "Yankee Doodle" chromo which had initially enabled him to move his family from Wellington to Cleveland. When this source of funds began to dry up, he expanded a small art club he had organized into the Cleveland Academy of Art. This group sponsored several art exhibitions, but its chief activity was providing art instruction. Willard's frequent changes of residence during the 1880s may have been influenced by the changing conditions of Cleveland's rapid growth, but they were more probably due to his dwindling income. The mid-1890s found the artist in failing health and in such need of financial assistance that a bill was proposed to the state legislature that he be commissioned to construct a monument of "The Spirit of '76" in Wellington.

Fortunately this marked the bottom of Willard's decline. Reverend William E. Barton, the father of the advertising executive Bruce Barton, began to take an interest in the artist, whom he had gotten to know during the two years he spent in Wellington. He published several promotional pieces on Willard, including one in the July 1898 issue of *Success* magazine, and provided him with the job of illustrating his children's book, *The Story of a Pumpkin Pie*.

Willard's real savior, however, was war. In 1895, Ryder wrote to Barton that the publication of Willard's work "has long been discontinued and the subjects out of print,"[35] but shortly after the outbreak of the Spanish American War he proclaimed, "We are in 'Yankee Doodle' times again and Willard has lost nothing in his power to excite patriotic stir with his good right hand."[36] Ryder may have been referring to an illustration Willard did for the Cleveland *Plain Dealer* of the American troops being led to Havana by his fifer and two drummers, but Ryder also must have sensed the renewed interest in the picture itself, which began to appear in grade school textbooks and to be featured as a bonus in advertisements.

This revival was nothing like that which World War I brought. While Pershing's proclamation, "Lafayette, we are here" rang through the air, magazines and newspapers began featuring "The Spirit of '76" as the pictorial embodiment of these words. One of the several articles on Willard which came out during these years asserted that the "Spirit of '76" would "pictorially become in patriotic American sentiment what 'The Battle Hymn of the Republic' already was in song ... [his trio] have become symbols of a spirit that is as fervently strong as it was in the earlier days."[37] Willard was invited to Chicago to speak and ride in parades. Shortly thereafter he died, and as he passed to the grave and oblivion his picture was ushered into the pantheon of American popular culture.

In view of the dark shadow "The Spirit of '76" cast over Willard's subsequent life, it is hardly surprising that the painting also preempted its creator in all accounts of Willard which extend beyond the Centennial. After the Exhibition, Willard arranged an extended tour for the picture which took it to Boston, Chicago, San Francisco, and eventually back to Boston. Finally from the fall of 1879 to the spring of 1880 it was put on display in the Corcoran Gallery in Washington. The main purpose of this tour was to capitalize on the picture's fame and arrange a lucrative sale. Unlike the inexpensive chromos, however, the large painting attracted few buyers. Finally Col.

[35] Letter dated March 30, 1895 (H.M.L.).

[36] Letter dated May 18, 1898 (H.M.L.).

[37] James H. Kennedy, " 'Yankee Doodle' in Paint," *Everybody's Magazine,* 37 (July 1917), 13. See also "America's Most Popular Picture," *Ladies Home Journal* (April 1919).

John Henry Devereux, the father of the boy who posed for the drummer, came forth in 1880 and offered a sum which was variously stated as high as $5,000 and as low as $1,500, the actual figure most probably having been nearer the $1,500. He then donated the picture to his hometown of Marblehead.

While the painting was in Boston, its name was changed to the "Spirit of '76." This is said to have been done because a local halfwit had the nickname of "Yankee Doodle."[38] However, it seems more probable that Willard was persuaded to make this switch by reactions such as that of the reviewer in the *Boston Evening Traveler* who observed that "the picture will be greeted by Americans as a genuine exponent of the spirit of '76."[39] Such was the beginning of a whole series of changes that have come to be associated with the painting. On one hand the Marblehead "Spirit" is so large that one scholar has expressed doubt that it could ever have been painted in the small studio Willard was using at the time. When the painting was returned to Cleveland for extensive repairs in 1892, according to this theory, Willard substituted a larger painting in which he modified the foreground cannon Devereux thought offensively large. As a result of this turn of affairs, the Western Reserve Historical Society fell heir to the original, its reduced size, extensive damage, and prominent cannon proclaiming its authenticity.[40] In 1962, Rip Pratt, a travel writer, reinforced this argument when he discovered that the postcard reproduction being sold in Abbot Hall was not the same picture as the one hanging on display. Additional investigation traced this postcard to a photograph taken by a local photographer in 1915.[41] Unwittingly the Marblehead Historical Society further added to these growing doubts by adamantly refusing for years to allow the picture to be photographed or closely examined.[42]

Like so much of the published information about Willard's life, this controversy springs largely from whimsical imaginings and carelessness. Willard, Ryder, and Devereux contribute no support for such an exchange. Moreover, in 1895 Ryder opened a new gallery, and Willard presented him with a copy of the "Spirit" which was to hang, along with other works contributed by artists he had promoted, in a sizeable area of wall space between the ceiling and a lower division of molding. The "Spirit" in the Western Reserve Historical Society came from Ryder's shop, its size corresponding to the dimensions of this designated space as both it and the cir-

---

[38] Devereux, 35–36.

[39] Quoted in an article in *Cleveland Voice* (Jan. 28, 1877).

[40] Benton, 80–83.

[41] Rip Pratt, "The Duplicate in Abbot Hall," *Yankee* (Sept. 1962), 52–56, 94–96.

[42] An article in the Aug. 12, 1935, issue of *Time* discusses the very strict prohibition against photographing the Marblehead picture that had been in effect for the past fifty years (p. 39). As recently as last year, a visiting scholar was denied access to the picture.

cumstances of the presentation were described in a letter by Ryder to Barton.[43] There is even a picture showing exactly how the picture was hung.[44] Pratt's findings, by placing the change sometime after 1915, actually add little support to the theory of the 1892 switch. Also had he researched his photo a bit more carefully, he would have discovered that it was not a picture of another painting but was rather a copy of either the original chromolithograph or the cabinet photo of it Ryder had once sold.

For me, however, the original will always be the chromolithograph which is now in storage in the Library of Congress. This predated either of the paintings in Cleveland and Marblehead and was the original source for the painting as well as its fame. It best embodied the beliefs of both the artist and the man who promoted it. The once gaudy, now faded colors of this chromo are the perfect complement to the picture's atmosphere of martial music, pretentious patriotism, and resolute determination that had so little to do with the actual Revolution but were the quintessential spirit of industrial America in 1876. It also illustrates the often misunderstood fact of popular culture that the fame of a particular product may depend as much upon the process of its creation and distribution as its content. James Ryder possessed a keen understanding of the complex relationship between art and photography and saw a unique opportunity for capitalizing on the enormous popularity of chromolithography. With his eye closely trained on the shifting conditions of the age in which he lived, he cultivated the unrealized penchant for the past in both Willard and the American public. Though Ryder too has been forgotten, each new adaptation of "The Spirit of '76" that promotes another consumer product unwittingly pays tribute to the spirit of enterprise he embodied in the very process of evoking the false sense of grandeur which eventually destroyed Archibald Willard.

[43]Letter dated Oct. 16, 1895 (H.M.I..).
[44]Held in collection of Willard materials at Western Reserve Historical Society.

WORDS AS SOCIAL CONTROL: NOAH WEBSTER AND THE CREATION OF THE *AMERICAN DICTIONARY*

RICHARD M. ROLLINS
Ohio State University

"I FINISHED WRITING MY DICTIONARY IN JANUARY, 1825," Noah Webster once recalled. It was a solemn moment:

> When I had come to the last word, I was seized with a trembling which made it somewhat difficult to hold my pen steady for writing. The cause seems to have been the thought that I might not then live to finish the work, or the thought that I was so near the end of my labors. But I summoned the strength to finish the last word, and then walking about the room a few minutes I recovered.[1]

So ended twenty-five years of constant, daily labor. The finished product was, by all standards, a monumental achievement. With 70,000 entries, all written out by his own hand, it was a massive work, the last major dictionary ever compiled by a single individual.[2] It has become, in the form of its successors, an integral part of American culture. As early as the mid-nineteenth century the name Webster had become synonymous with a dictionary.[3]

Virtually everyone believes that the *American Dictionary of the English Language* was a nationalistic tract. So pervasive is this belief that many historians, like Oscar Handlin and John D. Hicks, discuss the work in the context of rising nationalism without really stating that the work was thus

---

[1]Undated quote in Emily E. F. Ford, *Notes on the Life of Noah Webster* (New York: Private Printing, 1912), Vol. I, 293.

[2]Robert Keith Leavitt, *Noah's Ark: New England Yankees and the Endless Quest* (Springfield, Mass.: G. and C. Merriam Company, 1947).

[3]Horace E. Scudder, *Noah Webster* (Boston: Houghton Mifflin, 1888).

motivated.[4] They write as if Webster's nationalism was common knowledge and that there could be no other explanation for his work. Others have made clearer statements concerning the subject. Charles Beard called the dictionary a high note of nationalism;[5] Merle Curti and his associates portrayed it as a patriotic effort,[6] while John Krout and Dixon Ryan Fox fit it nicely into their narrative of the completion of American Independence.[7] Even Lawrence J. Friedman, who correctly notes Webster's alienation, portrays the dictionary as a patriotic work.[8] Those who have concentrated on Webster or the dictionary itself have been even more adamant in their conclusions. Homer D. Babbidge represents the attitude and methodology most commentators employ. He consistently confuses Webster's nationalistic statements of the 1780s with his later work, as if nothing occurred between 1783 and 1841.[9]

Nationalism is too simple an explanation. When the work is considered within the context of Noah Webster's life, it becomes apparent that it was stimulated by much more than patriotism. That was undoubtedly an important factor in his early conceptions, but the *American Dictionary* was the product of a lifetime. It reflected the events and inheritances of that human life and contained all the biases, concerns, and ideals of a specific individual. Indeed, it was an extension of his whole personality, and one must read it carefully to understand the tale it tells. Webster's main motivation for writing and publishing it was not to celebrate American life or to expand independence. Instead, he sought to counteract social disruption and reestablish the deferential world order that he believed was disintegrating.

* * *

Over the course of his eighty-four years, Noah Webster changed from an optimistic revolutionary in the 1780s, convinced that man could perfect himself and that America was the site of a future utopia,[10] to a pessimistic

[4]Oscar Handlin, *The History of the United States* (New York: Holt, Rinehart and Winston, 1967), Vol. I, 393, and John D. Hicks, George E. Mowry and Robert L. Burke, *A History of American Democracy*, 3rd ed. (Boston: Houghton Mifflin, 1966), 185.

[5]Charles A. Beard, *The Rise of American Civilization* (New York: Macmillan, 1940), 766.

[6]Merle Curti, Richard H. Shryock, Thomas C. Cochran, and Fred Harvey Harrington, *A History of American Civilization* (New York: Harper, 1953), 165.

[7]John A. Krout and Dixon Ryan Fox, *The Completion of American Independence, 1790–1830* (New York: Quadrangle, 1944), 33.

[8]Lawrence J. Friedman, *Inventors of the Promised Land* (New York: Knopf, 1975), 30–41.

[9]Homer D. Babbidge, Jr., ed., *Noah Webster: On Being American, Selected Writings, 1783–1828* (New York: Praeger, 1967). See also Harry R. Warfel, *Noah Webster: Schoolmaster to America* (New York: Octagon, 1936), 353.

[10]Webster also advocated universal white male suffrage, complete religious toleration, equal distribution of property (including confiscation of landed estates), and the abolition of slavery. For an analysis of Webster's writings in relation to revolutionary ideology as outlined by

critic of man and society. His buoyant nationalism dissolved under the
pressures of the events of the 1780s and 1790s. The question that commanded his attention during the last fifty years of his life was the conflict
between freedom and order. As with many others who perceived themselves
as America's moral stewards after 1800, his answer to that problem was
that all Americans should submit their hearts and minds to an authoritarian
God and mold themselves in the image of Quiet Christians. Good citizens
were not disruptive; they were obedient to the wishes of a social leadership
consisting of pious, elderly property owners. Webster's definitions of words,
both in his private correspondence and in the dictionary itself, as well as his
method of etymology, reflect this view. If Americans would only see the
world through the eyes and mind of Noah Webster as set forth in his dictionary, Christian peace and tranquillity would reign. Webster's main motivation was social control, and his dictionary was a means of achieving it.

The change in Webster began in the 1780s. Dissent in Connecticut, Shays'
Rebellion in Massachusetts, chaotic election procedures in the South, and
economic instability convinced him that an authority capable of enforcing
order was necessary, that the Articles of Confederation must be replaced. In
1787, the Pennsylvania delegation to the Constitutional Convention asked
him to write a defense of the new government. Webster happily complied,
expressing his view of the new system as a balance between revolutionary
ideals and social stability.[11]

The development of Webster's interest in language coincided with an
emerging emphasis on order. Throughout his life he exhibited a dualistic attitude toward language. It was a subject worthy of study by all Americans
for its own sake, but also a means to a greater end. In 1789 he published the
first significant American essay on linguistics, *Dissertations on the English
Language. . . .*[12] His concept of language as a tool of social change had
emerged. Webster believed that cultural as well as political independence
was necessary for the new nation to survive. Like Schlegel, Grimm, Horne
Tooke, and other Europeans, Webster believed that a connection between

---

Bernard Bailyn and Gordon S. Wood, see Richard M. Rollins, "Noah Webster: Propagandist
for the Revolution," *Connecticut History,* forthcoming, or Richard M. Rollins, "The Long
Journey of Noah Webster" (Diss., Michigan State University, 1976). The best source of information on Webster's early life is an unpublished autobiographical fragment: [Noah
Webster], "Memoir of Noah Webster," Webster Family Papers, Box 1, Yale Univ. Archives.
For a complete listing of all his work, see Edwin A. Carpenter, ed., *A Bibliography of the Writings of Noah Webster* (New York: New York Public Library, 1958).

[11][Noah Webster], *An Examination into the Leading Principles of the Federal Constitution
. . .* (Philadelphia: Pritchard and Hill, 1787). See also Webster's *Diary,* The Papers of Noah
Webster, Manuscripts and Archives, New York Public Library (archive hereafter cited as
NYPL).

[12]Noah Webster, *Dissertations on the English Language . . .* (Boston: Isaiah Thomas and
Company, 1789).

language and the nation existed. "A *national language* is a bond of *national union*," he said, and it should "be employed to render the people of this country national. . . ."[13]

Yet Webster's anxiety increased in response to the events of the 1790s. The growth of the democratic societies, mob violence, the activities of Genêt and his supporters, and especially the political battles and public vituperation dismayed him. The terror in France was a turning point. Shocked by the widespread use of the guillotine, Webster became convinced that man was innately depraved and that the expansion of human freedom and self-reliance brought only anarchy, chaos, murder, and brutality. Events in France seemed a portent of America's future, and thus he opposed efforts at progressive social change. The great experiment had produced only a people characterized by corruption, vice, deceit, and debauchery.[14]

On July Fourth of 1798 Webster gave an oration in New Haven in which he summarized the events of the previous twenty years and predicted the nation's future. It amounted to little more than a call for imposition of authority and a means of enforcing its wishes. Utopia had become a frightening den of iniquity; agitation and dissent must cease, a source of cohesion must be found. "Let us never forget that the cornerstone of all republican government is," he said, "that the will of every citizen is controlled by the laws of supreme will of the state."[15]

His criticism of the developing nation after 1798 was profound. The concept of equality seemed fallacious,[16] and democracy threatened civilization itself.[17] Only fatherly figures of authority could be trusted to govern. People would be freer and happier "if all were deprived of the right of suffrage until they were forty-five years of age, and if no man was eligible to an important office until he was fifty. . . ." All power should be vested in "our old men, who have lost their ambitions chiefly and have learnt wisdom by experience."[18]

Conversion to evangelical Protestantism in 1808 provided Webster with more detailed explanations of all his fears. With men like John Jay, Stephen Van Rensselaer, Timothy Dwight, John Cotton Smith, and Elias Boudinot, Webster believed that religion provided the only viable basis for civilization. They saw themselves as "their brother's keepers," and were determined to

[13]Ibid., 397. Webster's use of italics is inconsistent throughout his dictionary.
[14]See especially Letter To Timothy Pickering, July 7, 1797, Ford, *Notes,* I, 422 and *Minerva,* July 12, Aug. 14, 1797.
[15]Noah Webster, "An Oration, Pronounced before the Citizens of New Haven . . . ," *Commercial Advertiser,* July 24, 1798.
[16]Noah Webster, *An Oration, Pronounced before the Citizens of New Haven, on the Anniversary of the Declaration of Independence; July, 1802* (New Haven: William W. Morse, 1802), 16.
[17]Letter to Oliver Wolcott, Sept. 16, 1800, *Ford,* I, 504 06.
[18]Letter to Benjamin Rush, Dec. 15, 1800, ibid., 479.

oversee America's return to tranquillity through their own moral stewardship. They formed large organizations, including the American Bible Society, the American Tract Society, and the American Sunday School Union
in order to spread their doctrines of Quiet Christian deference and to
enhance public acquiescence.[19] In everything he wrote after 1808, from or-
dinary school books to evangelical tracts and including his own version of the
Holy Bible, Webster proclaimed that fearful worship of God was the first
step to civil order, that government should be run by the elderly, pious, and
wealthy. He summed up his conception of the influence of religion on behavior and society:

> Real religion implies a habitual sense of divine presence, and a fear of offending the
> Supreme Being, subdues and controls all the turbulent passions; and nothing is
> seen in the Christian, but meekness, forbearance, and kindness, accompanied by a
> serenity of mind and a desire to please, as uniform as they are cheering to families
> and friends.[20]

Americans should not agitate for social change but must instead be
obedient followers of the law as laid down by the moral stewards. All would
be chaos without total obedience to God:

> . . . we are cast on the ocean of life, without chart, or compass, or rudder—nay, we
> are ignorant of our own port—we know not where we are bound—we have not a
> ray of light to guide us in the tempestuous sea—not a hope to cheer us amidst the
> distresses of this world, or tranquillize the soul in its passage into the next—and all
> beyond the present state, is annihilation or despair![21]

In this frame of mind, far from one of exuberant nationalism, Webster wrote
his dictionary.

[19] Several studies of the religious benevolence movement in the early nineteenth century have
been written. Most stress the social control aspect; these include Clifford S. Griffin, *Their
Brother's Keepers: Moral Stewardship in the United States, 1815–1865* (New Brunswick: Rut-
gers Univ. Press, 1964), and "Religious Benevolence as Social Control, 1815–1860," *Mississippi
Valley Historical Review,* 64 (Dec. 1957), 423–44; Stephen E. Berk, *Calvinism versus
Democracy: Timothy Dwight and the Origins of American Evangelical Orthodoxy* (Hamden,
Conn.: Archon Books, 1974); M. J. Heale, "Humanitarianism in the Early Republic: The Moral
Reformers of New York, 1776–1825," *Journal of American Studies,* 2 (Oct. 1968), 161–75; W.
David Lewis, "The Reformers as Conservatives: Protestant Counter-Subversion in the Early
Republic," in Stanley Coben and Lorman Ratner, eds., *The Development of an American Cul-
ture* (Englewood Cliffs, N.J.: Prentice-Hall, 1970); and Raymond A. Mohl, *Poverty in New
York, 1783–1825* (New York: Oxford Univ. Press, 1970). For a skeptical analysis, see Lois W.
Banner, "Religious Benevolence as Social Control: A Critique of an Interpretation," *Journal of
American History,* 60 (June 1973), 23–41.
[20] Noah Webster, *Letter from Noah Webster, Esq., of New Haven, Connecticut, to a friend in
Explanation and Defense of the Distinguishing Doctrines of the Gospel* (New York: J. Seymour,
1809), 22.
[21] Noah Webster, "Letter to a Young Gentleman Commencing his Education," *A Collection
of Papers on Political, Literary and Moral Subjects* (New York: Webster and Clark, 1843), 86.
This essay was first published in 1823.

It is natural to draw direct links between Webster's early nationalism and his *American Dictionary*. And of course Webster encouraged this in the title and in his preface to his most famous work. He noted that the chief glory of a nation arose from its authors and stated that American writers were equal to Englishmen. He even named those on this side of the Atlantic whom he considered comparable to the best of Europe. Franklin, Washington, Adams, Jay, Madison, Marshall, Dwight, Trumbull, and Irving were his more well-known favorites. Nonetheless, the nationalist context is insufficient to explain the book. Perhaps as an indication of what was to come, Webster did not mention the internationally famous American who symbolized all that he loathed, Thomas Jefferson. Thomas Paine and other earlier American celebrators of democracy and freedom were also neglected. As George Krapp, the most respected twentieth-century student of the development of the English language has noted, merely naming Franklin, Washington, and others as authorities "is quite a different matter from the narrow patriotic zeal which was rampant in the years immediately following the Revolution."[22]

In addition, Webster himself indicated that his views had changed. "It is not only important, but, in a degree necessary," he said in the opening pages, "that the people of this country, should have an *American Dictionary* of the English language. . . ." He did not advocate the development of a new language, or even a new dialect. Instead, he perceived himself to be writing merely an "American" dictionary of the English language, which is different from creating a whole new language. And he further explained his position, noting that the body of the language was basically the same as that of England. He added a revealing statement: "It is desirable to perpetuate that sameness."[23]

Thus the end product of Webster's toils was anything but a new "American tongue." He included only about fifty Americanisms, a fact which prompted H. L. Mencken to label Webster an incompetent observer of his own country.[24] The lexicographer's nationalism had in fact reached a low point in 1814, when he helped draft the first circular calling for the Hartford Convention.[25] In that year he also denounced the Constitution as naive and wildly democratic, ridiculed the concept of universal white male suffrage, and called for division of the union into three separate countries.[26]

[22]George Phillip Krapp, *The English Language in America* (New York: Ungar, 1925), 338.
[23]Noah Webster, *An American Dictionary of the English Language* . . . (New York: S. Converse, 1828), [iii]. Hereafter cited as *A. D.*
[24]H. L. Mencken, *The American Language: An Inquiry into the Development of English in the United States* (New York: Knopf, 1923), 42.
[25]From Joseph Lyman, Jan. 5, 1814, Ford, *Notes*, II, 124. Carpenter, *Bibliography*, 363, indicates that Webster was the author of this letter.
[26]Noah Webster, *An Oration, Pronounced Before the Knox and Warren Branches of the Washington Benevolence Society, at Amherst* . . . (Northampton, Mass.: William Butler, 1814).

The *American Dictionary* was perfectly acceptable in England. The first edition of 2,500 copies was quickly followed by an English edition of 3,000, and one major student of lexicography had noted that Webster's crowning achievement was quite suitable for use in America and England.[27] Indeed, his dictionary was received more warmly across the Atlantic than in the United States. Warfel stated that "soon Webster became the standard in England. . . ." When his publisher went bankrupt, copies of the English edition were sold without change in America.[28]

Yet another incident suggests that his dictionary was not a nationalistic tract. When the second American edition was published in 1841, he sent a copy to Queen Victoria. Significantly, he told the person carrying it to her that "our common language is one of the ties that binds the two nations together; I hope the works I have executed will manifest to the British nation that the Americans are not willing to suffer it to degenerate on this side of the Atlantic."[29] Half a century earlier he had despised England and all that it stood for. Now he told the Queen that he hoped his dictionary might furnish evidence that the "genuine descendants of English ancestors born on the west of the Atlantic, have not forgotten either the land or the language of their fathers."[30]

* * *

Webster made his intentions in the dictionary explicit. The values expressed within the work were his. "In many cases, I have given brief sentences of my own," he declared, "and often presenting some important maxim or sentiment in religion, morality, law or civil policy. . . ."[31]

While Webster's work in etymology exhibited the influence of his social and political values, he sincerely believed that it was new, scholarly, and in fact the most important part of his work. As Laird correctly notes, of all the causes he supported over his long life, and they were legion, "none was dearer to him than was the pursuit of etymologies, and in nothing so much as in his vast synopsis of 'language affinities' . . . did he repose his hopes for the gratitude and admiration of society."[32] As early as 1806 Webster had vowed to "make one effort to dissolve the chains of illusions" surrounding the development of language.[33] A year later he had begun to compile the dic-

[27]George H. McKnight, *The Evolution of the English Language: From Chaucer to the Twentieth Century* (New York: Dover, 1968).

[28]Warfel, *Webster,* 361, 365.

[29]Letter to Andrew Stevenson, June 22, 1841, The Papers of Noah Webster, Box 1, NYPL.

[30]Letter to Her Majesty, Victoria, Queen of Great Britain, June 22, 1841, The Papers of Noah Webster, Box 1, NYPL.

[31]*A. D.* n. p.

[32]Charlton Laird, "Etymology, Anglo-Saxon, and Noah Webster," *American Speech* (Feb. 1946), 3.

[33]Noah Webster, *A Compendious Dictionary of the English Language . . .* (New Haven: Hudson and Goodwin, 1806), xxiii.

tionary by concentrating merely on definitions and correcting errors in orthography. This had led him "gradually and almost insensibly" to investigate the origin of the English language. He had been surprised to learn that the path of development of all European languages was an unexplored subject. All other etymologists had "wandered into the field of conjecture, venturing to substitute opinions for evidence. . . ."[34] By 1809 he had concluded that language had begun in Asia and migrated outward.[35] At about this time, Webster stopped working on definitions and orthography and spent ten years compiling his synopsis of the affinities of languages,[36] on which his etymology in his dictionary was based. Four years before his death he still believed that his work was superior to any others and that any other etymology, including those by "the German scholars, the most accurate philologists in Europe, appears to be wholly deficient."[37]

Yet, according to modern etymologists, it was Webster who was in error, not the Europeans. In fact, his etymology has been judged a failure.[38] George Krapp has come close to explaining Webster's errors. "In short," he said, "it was really spiritual, not phonological truth in which Webster was primarily interested." He seems to have thought "that the truth of a word, that is the primitive and original radical value of the word, was equivalent to the truth of the idea."[39]

Webster's etymology was a literal extrapolation of Scriptural truth, the only concrete truth, as far as he was concerned, into another field. Since 1808 he had believed that the Bible was factually correct, and that it must be accepted as such. Without it, there was no basis for civilization itself. Thus his rejection of European etymologists is no mystery. Their scientific attempts to unravel the development of language led away from the story of the Tower of Babel. They were challenging the validity of the Bible, the only rock upon which peace and tranquillity could be secured.

In 1806, as he began his etymological studies, Webster commented specifically on this subject. He believed that etymology illuminated not just the origins of words but the development of human history as well. The etymology of the languages of Europe "will throw no inconsiderable light on the origin and history of the several nations who people it, and confirm in no small degree, the scriptures account of the dispersion of men."[40]

[34]"To the Friends of Literature in the United States," Harry R. Warfel, *The Letters of Noah Webster* (New York: Library Publishers, 1953), 272.

[35]Letter to Thomas Dawes, July 25, 1809, ibid., 343.

[36]Letter to John Jay, Nov., 1821, *Ford,* II, 160–61.

[37]Noah Webster, *Observations on Language* . . . (New York: S. Babcock, 1839), 5.

[38]Webster's etymology has been heavily criticized by nearly all experts in the field. The most recent and thorough student of lexicography, Joseph Friend, *The Development of American Lexicography,* 1798–1864 (Paris: Mouton, 1967), summarizes their analyses.

[39]Krapp, *Language,* 365.

[40]Webster, *Compendious Dictionary,* xix.

In the final analysis, Webster had no choice but to write Christian etymology, regardless of the methodology and insights of other authors. The only ultimate truth was contained in the Scriptures, and it dictated the mere truth of words. Beside Christ, Schlegel and Grimm were insignificant. They challenged the validity of Christianity, and if the authority of the Scriptures was demolished, there was simply no hope for mankind. Without literal belief in Biblical truth, he said in 1823, "we are cast on the ocean of life, without chart, or compass, or rudder." Only "annihilation and despair" could result if the Scriptures were found invalid in any area.[41] Given this vision, Webster was incapable of seeing the development of language in any framework of explanation other than that set forth in the Bible.

Webster introduced his etymology with a literal belief in the origin of language according to Genesis. Vocal sounds, he noted, were used to communicate between Adam and Eve. "Hence we may infer that language was bestowed on Adam, in the same manner as all his other faculties and knowledge, by supernatural power; or in other words was of divine origin. . . ." "It is therefore probable that *language* as well as the faculty of speech, was the immediate gift of God."[42] Webster then traced the Biblical story of the development of man, which was the basis for all the deviations of the words in the two volumes.[43] As Joseph Friend notes, no amount of hard work, not even the labor of a quarter of a century, could overcome the limitations imposed by this Scriptural literalism.[44] He accepted without question the story of the Tower of Babel and the confusion of tongues. Before that time all mankind had spoken a common language, which Webster called "Chaldee," and which modern etymologists agree was a fantasy. When those in Babel were dispersed, they divided into three groups, each led by a son of Noah: Shem, Ham, and Japheth. The last had eventually migrated to Northern Europe, and thus all the languages of that area were labeled "Japhetic." This development, believed Webster, could be traced through the existence of certain words that reappeared in several languages, as well as through the existence of words with similar construction and meaning in various languages.

One example of Webster's etymology will illustrate both his change in viewpoint over time and his authoritarian cast of mind. In 1789 he had remarked that the word "God" had come from the concept "good," and that His nature was the explanation of that derivation.[45] In 1826 he specifically rejected that idea. Instead, he noted that "Supreme Being" was taken from

[41]Webster, "Young Gentleman," 86.
[42]Letter to David McClure, Oct. 25, 1836, Warfel, *Letters*, 454.
[43]*A. D.*, (vii).
[44]Friend, *Development*, 76.
[45]Webster, *Dissertations*, 399.

"supremacy or power." Thus "God" was "equivalent to lord or ruler, from some root signifying to press or exert force."[46]

* * *

In attempting to understand the *American Dictionary* and the man who wrote it, we must recall that Webster's view of language was dualistic. It was, of course, to be studied for its own sake, but it was also something much more. Language, he believed, influenced opinion and behavior. If people had a clear understanding of "equality," they would act in certain ways. Language could be used as a means to a greater end. It could be altered and manipulated, and in so doing, one could affect millions of people. Although he never explicitly said so, Webster assumed this from the very beginning of his work. It is implicit in his early attempts—later repudiated—to forge an "American tongue" as a way of encouraging independence from a vile and corrupt England, and to further his utopian dreams. Even in 1788 he could conceptualize the use of language in purifying society. In that year he called for studies which would "show how far truth and accuracy of thinking are concerned in a clear understanding of *words*." Language should be studied "if it can be proved that *mere use of words* has led nations into error, and still continues the delusion. . . ."[47] As early at 1790 he was engaged in manipulation of language as a means of influencing opinion and behavior. He had just completed another book, he told a friend. "I have introduced into it some definitions, relative to the slave trade," he said, "calculated to impress upon young minds the detestableness of the trade."[48]

Webster's disillusionment with man and society was accompanied by the conclusion that the definition of words played a role in American development. "There is one remarkable circumstance in our own history which seems to have escaped observation," he noted in 1838, "which is, the mischievous effect of the indefinite application of terms." A year later he wrote an essay in which he summed up his entire life's work in linguistics, philology, etymology, and lexicography. "It is obvious to my mind, that popular errors proceeding from a misunderstanding of words," he said, "are among the efficient causes of our political disorders. . . ."[49]

The thought process which led to etymological error also led to certain definitions. His correspondence and publications offer the opportunity to ob-

[46]*A. D.*
[47]Noah Webster, "A Dissertation concerning the influence of Language on opinions and of opinions on Language," *American Magazine* (May 1788), 399.
[48]Letter to J. Pemberton, March 15, 1790, Historical Society of Pennsylvania Archives.
[49]Noah Webster, *Observations,* 31–32.

serve the way in which definitions were formed. Indeed, examples of the
influence of social events and opinions abound, including the formulation of
definitions which appeared almost intact decades later in his dictionaries.
They reveal that his strong social and political values and his longing for
public submission to authority dictated what he believed should be the correct understanding of important words.

He wrote that an incorrect understanding of the word "pension" had been
partially responsible for social discord in the 1780s. Congress had granted a
pension to officers who had served in the Continental Army. Many had
protested, and a convention held in Middletown, Connecticut, had called for
its repeal. This unrest had distressed Webster. It had been "a remarkable,
but unfortunate instance of the use of the word, in a sense so indefinite that
the people at large made no distinction between *pensions* granted as a provi-
sion for old officers, and *pensions* granted for the purpose of bribery for
favor and support." Obviously Webster thought that the half-pay for officers
was the first type of pension, while to the convention it was the second kind.
In his dictionary he was careful to say that it meant "to grant an annual
allowance from the public treasury to a person for past services. . . ." No
example of the misunderstanding of words, he noted, was as important as
that surrounding the phrase "union of church and state." He understood the
aversion of many Americans to the unification of ecclesiastical and civil authority because of the European experience. Along with many others,
Webster had spoken in favor of their separation in the 1780s. But times had
changed, and by 1838 his conception of that relationship had also changed.
Now the union of the two meant that "all laws must have *religion for their
basis.*" In this sense, there was a strong need for a "union of civil and ecclesiastical powers; in support of the laws and institutions."[50] This union was
the seedbed of Quiet Christians and the heart of his concept of social relations.

"Jacobinism," "democrat," and "republican" were prominent words that
Webster's biases led him to define in significant ways. The first, he said in
1799, was not merely the philosophy of a French political faction. It was
instead "an opposition to established government and institutions, and an attempt to overthrow them, by private accusations or by violent or illegal
means."[51] "Democrat" was "synonymous with the word *Jacobian* in
France. . . ." Democratic organizations arose from the attempt to "control
our government by private associations." By 1800 the word signified "a
person who attempts undue opposition to our influence over government by
means of private clubs, secret intrigues, or by public popular meetings which

[50]*Middletown* (Conn.) *Constitution,* Dec. 5, 1838.
[51]*Commercial Advertiser,* Oct. 21, 1799.

are extraneous to the Constitution."[52] "Republicans," on the other hand, were "friends of our Representative Governments, who believe that no influence whatever should be exercised in a state which is directly authorized by and developed by legislation."[53] Similar definitions appeared in his dictionary.

A key word, the definition of which he felt could influence action, was "free." Most Americans were convinced that all men were free to act according to their own wills. The idea that this abstract condition was natural and was a basic part of American life was widely upheld, or so thought Noah Webster. To him it was absurd, and in fact "contributed to the popular licentiousness, which often disturbs the public peace, and even threatens extensive evils in this country." A misunderstanding of "free" threatened the permanency of government, because it led people to feel that somehow individuals were "*above* the constitutional authorities."[54] It was also simply incorrect. Instead, all individuals, from the time of their birth, were subject to the demands of their parents, of God, and of the government of the country in which they lived.[55] There would be fewer problems in society, said Noah Webster, if Americans understood that "*No person is born free,* in the general acception of the word *free.*"[56]

"Equality" and "equal" were also crucial terms. "Nothing can be more obvious than that by the appointment of the creator, in the constitution of man and of human society," he wrote a few months before his death, "the conditions of men must be different and *unequal.*"[57] The common American assumption that all men must be equal in conditions in which they lived was false. The Declaration of Independence was wrong when it began by affirming as a self-evident truth that "all men are born *equal.*" That was the work of the infamous idealist, Thomas Jefferson, and as a universal proposition had to be rejected. In their intellectual and physical powers men were born "*unequal,*" and hence inequality was a basic part of human life. Webster said that most of the men of the earlier generation had maintained that each person was born with an "equal natural right to liberty and protection. . . ," something far different than total equality, an idea that led to agitation over the right of suffrage.[58] The founders had believed in equality of opportunity, with which Webster had no argument. "But *equality of condition* is a very different thing and dependent on circumstances over which government and laws have no control."[59]

[52] Letter to Joseph Priestley, 1800, Warfel, *Letters,* 208.
[53] Ibid., 207–08.
[54] *Middletown Constitution,* Dec. 5, 1838.
[55] Noah Webster, "Discourse delivered before the Connecticut Historical Society on April 21, 1840," 29, Connecticut Historical Society.
[56] Letter to Daniel Webster, n.d., Warfel, *Letters,* 482.
[57] Letter to James Kent, Feb. 7, 1843, The Papers of Noah Webster, Box 8, NYPL.
[58] *Commercial Advertiser,* Jan. 20, 1835.
[59] Webster, "Discourse," 30.

Most importantly, when people expected equality of condition, it led inevitably to opposition to authority, chaos, and ultimately anarchy. Misunderstanding of the words *"free* and *equal"* influenced "the more ignorant and turbulent part of the community" to become "emboldened" and to "take the law into their own hands, or to trample both constitution and law under their feet."[60] The very concept of equality of condition could culminate in disaster:

> . . . It is not for the interest and safety of society that all men should be equal. Perfect equality, if such a state could be supposed practicable, would render due subordination impossible, and dissolve society. All men in a community are equally entitled to protection, and the secure enjoyment of their rights. . . . Superiority in natural and acquired endowments, and in authority derived from the laws, is essential to the existence of social order, and of personal safety.[61]

In his dictionary Webster listed nineteen definitions of the words "equal" and "equality." His faith in equality among men is conspicuous only by its absence.

* * *

Webster's emphasis on Quiet Christian behavior appears throughout the definitions in the *American Dictionary* itself. The reader is reminded of his divinely-directed role in life and the values by which he should live. The fear of God, absolute and rigid controller of all things, the depravity of man, and the character traits of meekness, humility, passivity, and wholehearted submission to proper authority are celebrated in the definitions of hundreds and perhaps thousands of words. This was done in two ways: either through definitions outlining deferential conduct, or through quotes illustrating the meaning of the word. He defined "author," for instance, as "One who produces, creates, or brings into being. . . ." Webster could have stopped there, with an objective statement, as other lexicographers did. Instead he added "as, God is the *author* of the Universe," thus reminding the reader of His fearful power.[62]

Webster interjected his obsession with authority into the most intimate of human relationships. The verb form of "love" was "a sense to be pleased with," to which he added a significant set of examples of its usage, again designed to instruct the Quiet Christian:

> The Christian *loves* his Bible. In short, we *love* whatever gives us pleasure and de-

[60]*Middletown Constitution,* Dec. 5, 1838.

[61]Ibid.

[62]The *American Dictionary* was unpaginated, but definitions may be found in their correct alphabetical order. The original edition has recently been reissued: Rosalie Slater, ed., *Noah Webster's First Edition of an American Dictionary of the English Language* (Anaheim, California: Foundation for American Christian Education, 1967).

light, whether animal or intellectual; and if our hearts are right, we *love* God above all things, as the sum of all excellence and all the attributes which can communicate happiness to intelligent beings. In other words, the Christian *loves* God with the love of complacency in his attributes, the love of benevolence towards the interests of his kingdom, and the love of gratitude for favors received.

The noun form of "love" was also used in a similar way. Webster gives another example of the use of religion in forming deferential, Quiet Christian personalities and demeanor:

The *love* of God is the first duty of man, and this springs from just views of his attributes or excellencies of character, which afford the highest delight to the sanctified heart. Esteem and reverence constitute ingredients in this affection, and a fear of offending him is the inseparable effect.

The dictionary also evidenced Webster's disgust with politicians and politics. He defined them as men "of artifice or deep contrivance" rather than people engaged in government or management of affairs. The adjective form of "politician" meant "cunning; using artifice." His own longing for a return to some former time before the rise of democratic politics was indicated in his definition of "polity." He quoted Ezra Stiles, who said, "were the whole Christian world to revert back to the original model, how far more simple, uniform and beautiful would the church appear, and how far more agreeable to the ecclesiastical *polity* instituted by the holy apostles."

The Quiet Christian image appears throughout the dictionary. "Laws" were "the *laws* which enjoin the duties of piety and morality, and prescribed by God and found in the Scriptures." Under "submission" Webster again insists that the Quiet Christian should be full of "resignation," meaning "entire and cheerful *submission* to the will of God [which] is a Christian duty of prime excellence." The only individual who could be "esteemed really and permanently happy" is the one "who enjoys a peace of mind in the favor of God," not unlike the mental tranquillity he had found in 1808. Defining "improve," he commands that "it is the duty . . . of a good man to *improve* in grace and piety." He tells us that "the distribution of the Scriptures may be the *instrument* of a vastly extensive reformation in morals and religion." Webster's view of the family appears in his definition of "marriage" as "instituted by God himself, for the sexes, for promoting domestic felicity and for securing the maintenance and education of children." The helplessness of a man is accented when he tells us under "meritorious" that "we rely for salvation on the *meritorious* obedience and suffering of Christ."

The dictionary is saturated with commands to be quiescent. Only a few examples will suffice as a general indication of the flavor of the work. "Good breeding forbids us to use *offensive* words." "A man is *profane* when he takes the name of God in vain, or treats sacred things with abuse and irreverence." "*Perfect rectitude* belongs only to the Supreme Being. The more nearly the *rectitude* of men approaches to the standard of divine law, the more exalted and dignified is their character. Want of *rectitude* is not only sinful, but debasing." "Freedom" is defined in one sense as "violation of the rules of decorum," while Webster warns us to "beware of what are called innocent *freedoms.*" Webster's denial of freedom and advocacy of submission to authority is consistent. "Freedom" in another sense is defined as "license."

"Duty" is a key concept, and in defining it Webster commands us to obey virtually any authority:

> That which a person owes to another; that which a person is bound, by any natural, moral or legal obligation, to pay, do or perform. Obedience to princes, magistrates and the laws is the *duty* of every citizen and subject; obedience, respect and kindness to parents are the *duties* of children; fidelity to friends is a *duty;* reverence, obedience and prayer to God are indisputable *duties*; the government and religious instruction of children are *duties* of parents which they cannot neglect without guilt.

"Submission" was synonymous with "obedience," and "*submission* of children to their parents is an indispensible duty." "Government" meant "control; restraint." In this definition he added that "Children are often ruined by a neglect of *government* in parents." Under "inferior" Webster commands us to "Pay due respect to those who are superior in station, and due civility to those who are *inferior.*"

"Liberty" is one of the most revealing terms in the *American Dictionary.* His first definition was simply "freedom from restraint. . . ." To this, however, he added some interesting distinctions. Most important were the two types of liberty that John Winthrop had spoken of in 1645. *"Natural liberty"* meant the "power of acting as one thinks fit, without any restraint or control, except from the laws of nature." Like Winthrop, he emphasized that this condition was impractical and was always "abridged by the establishment of government." He was not speaking of the Lockean notion of a government as a compact between men, but of the need for restraint on human liberty. *"Civil liberty,"* on the other hand, was the liberty "of men in a state of society" in which natural liberty was "abridged and restrained" not to enhance cooperation or distribution of goods, but for "the safety and interest of the society, state or nation." Civil liberty he stated was "secured by established laws, which restrain every man from injuring or controlling others." He was undoubtedly thinking of the turmoil since the 1780s when he noted that "the restraints of law are essential to *civil liberty.*"

Perhaps the most revealing definition in the entire two-volume work was that of "education." This one small paragraph in many ways summed up much of Webster's life. Education had always been of interest to him, not only for its own value, but as a means of social change of one sort or another. In the early 1780s it had been an instrument of increasing both cultural independence from England and reform as well, and these two motivations were behind his first attempt to Americanize the schools systematically. After

1808 Webster had seen schools as institutions for producing Quiet Christians, as a means of insuring tranquillity by teaching a specific form of conduct.[63] Through them discipline could be instilled and the unruly passions of men checked and limited. His definition of education did not stress the increase of learning, of understanding or comprehending the world. Value-laden words emphasizing this side of education appear only twice: "enlighten the understanding," and "arts and science." The second occurrence is almost thrown in as if an afterthought. But terms espousing authoritarian control appear nine times in the space of three sentences: "formation of manners," "discipline," "correct the temper," "form the manners and habits of youth," "fit them for usefulness in their future stations," "manners," "religious *education*," "immense responsibility," "duties." And this is not counting the use of "instruction," a term he chose instead of "learning" or other, less authority-laden terms. Finally, notice that an education in manners, arts and science is merely "important." A religious education, with all its overtones of the Quiet Christian, is "indispensible."

One last definition demonstrates the interrelationship between religion, politics, behavior, and language that existed in Webster's mind. Under "reason," he quotes an author who said "God brings good out of evil, and therefore it were but *reason* we should trust God to govern his own world." Implicit is the notion that man should follow God's laws, not his own reason. Thus reason was used to advocate its opposite.

* * *

Every phase of the *American Dictionary* affirms the author's concern with authority and social control; exuberant nationalism is absent. The same obsession appears in the dedication of the work. One might expect a man who labored for twenty-five years on a single book to acknowledge the role played by those who influenced him. Modern scholars usually mention the work of those who came before them or others in the field. But, of course, Webster could not do that. If Webster had been a strong nationalist, as most historians have said, one might expect long paeans to American freedom, or celebrations of the heroes of the Revolution. But the *American Dictionary* was a product of Webster's evolving ideas about America. The work exhibited the values and beliefs of the evangelical movement of the early nineteenth century whose major emphasis was limiting human actions, not of the nationalistic fervor of the late eighteenth century. In his dedication Webster said:

> To the great and benevolent Being, who during the preparation of this work, has sustained a feeble constitution, amidst obstacles and toils, disappointments, infirmities and depression; who has twice borne me and my manuscripts in safety across the Atlantic, and given me strength and resolution to bring the work to a close, I would present the tribute of my most grateful acknowledgments.[64]

[63]Noah Webster, *A Plea for a Miserable World* . . . (Boston: Ezra Lincoln, 1820).
[64]*A. D.*, (v).

UNCLE TOM RECONSTRUCTED:
A NEGLECTED CHAPTER IN THE
HISTORY OF A BOOK

THOMAS P. RIGGIO
University of Connecticut

NO AMERICAN NOVEL, NOT EVEN MOBY DICK, HAS SO DRAMATIC A HISTORY AS the one written by "the little woman who wrote the book that made this big war." Lincoln's witticism proved prophetic, as *Uncle Tom's Cabin* has occasioned an ongoing battle for over a century. A major critical effort of the last two decades has been the rescue of Mrs. Stowe's novel and, especially, of its chief character from the opprobrium that had befallen them. The debate is cultural as well as literary, and it centers on the evolving role of "Uncle Tom" as a key emblem in black American history. Edmund Wilson's *New Yorker* review of *Uncle Tom's Cabin* (1948) gave impetus to the task of revision, which was continued in the writing of, among others, Howard Mumford Jones, David Levin, Kenneth Lynn, Kenneth Rexroth, and Cushing Strout.[1] However varied in approach, these writers share one basic assumption: the accepted picture of "Uncle Tom" as the prototypical black American who is, in James Baldwin's words, "robbed of his humanity and divested of his sex,"[2] is not to be found in Mrs. Stowe's book. In defense of the novel, the revisionists shifted the responsibility for Uncle Tom's vulgar image to the popular Tom shows and the Tom plays of the

---

[1] Edmund Wilson, review of Modern Library edition of *Uncle Tom's Cabin, New Yorker* (Nov. 27, 1948), 126–33; Howard Mumford Jones, "Introduction" to *Uncle Tom's Cabin* (Columbus, Ohio: Merrill, 1969); David Levin, "American Fiction as Historical Evidence: Reflections on *Uncle Tom's Cabin*," *Negro American Literature Forum*, 5 (1971), 132–36, 154; Kenneth S. Lynn (ed.), *Uncle Tom's Cabin* (Cambridge: Bellknap Press, 1962); Kenneth Rexroth, "Uncle Tom's Cabin," *Saturday Review*, 52:2 (Jan. 11, 1969), 71; Cushing Strout, "*Uncle Tom's Cabin* and the Portent of Millenium," *Yale Review*, 57 (1968), 375–85.

[2] James Baldwin, "Everybody's Protest Novel," *Partisan Review*, 16:6 (June 1949), 581. In the last quarter century, the position that Baldwin represents has held its own alongside the revisionists' argument for *Uncle Tom*. See, for example, J. C. Furnas, *Goodbye to Uncle Tom* (New York: Sloane, 1956), passim; Herbert Hill, " 'Uncle Tom,' An Enduring American Myth," *The Crisis*, 72 (May 1965), 289–95; George M. Frederickson, *The Black Image in the White Mind* (New York: Harper & Row, 1971), 97–129.

late nineteenth and the twentieth centuries. Charles Foster voices the common strategy of this group, writing that ". . . the distorted image of an important American author persists" because the common mistake is one of "utterly confusing the book with the stage plays and the Tom shows."[3] Given the degrading nature of many Tom plays, such historical reductionism is understandable. But unfortunately it is now a critical commonplace that leaves all other avenues to Uncle Tom's fate in our time virtually unexplored. Indeed, the full picture has yet to be constructed of how a book whose avowed and successful purpose was to champion an oppressed people came to stand as a major symbol of that oppression. The objectives of this essay are, first, to examine an important but neglected link in the eccentric popular history of *Uncle Tom's Cabin,* namely, its role in Southern Reconstruction fiction and particularly in the work of Thomas Dixon; and, second, to spark a reconsideration of the Tom plays' role in the shaping of Uncle Tom's contemporary image.

* * *

William Faulkner confirmed the revisionist position when he said that Mrs. Stowe ". . . was writing about Uncle Tom as a human being—and Legree and Eliza as human beings, not as puppets."[4] By implication the "puppets" are all in the Tom shows. Faulkner, one suspects, knew better than most that the Tom plays account for only one source of the inhuman reputation of Mrs. Stowe's characters. Legree aside, the image of the obsequious black lackey who struts about chanting, "Yes massa, yes massa" coincides with the stereotyped black man whose roots cultural historians have traced back to antebellum Southern literature.[5] Originally, at least, the stereotype fitted into a larger matrix of ideas that we now refer to as the myth of the Old South.

Anyone who reads (or sees) that latter-day paean to the Old South, *Gone with the Wind,* knows that the Old South was both a pre-Civil War South and a lost Golden Age. Every schoolboy recognizes the trappings of the legend. There was, of course, a stately mansion, usually white and upheld handsomely by Corinthian columns, between which stood the Southern

[3]Charles Foster, *The Rungless Ladder: Harriet Beecher Stowe and New England Puritanism* (Durham: Duke Univ. Press, 1954), viii–ix.

[4]In Joseph L. Fant and Robert Ashley (eds.), *Faulkner at West Point* (New York: Vintage Books, 1969), 104.

[5]Cf. Francis Pendelton Gaines, *The Southern Plantation: A Study in the Development and Accuracy of a Tradition* (New York: Columbia Univ. Press, 1924); W. J. Cash, *The Mind of the South* (New York: Knopf, 1941); Kenneth S. Lynn, *Mark Twain and Southwestern Humor* (Boston: Little, Brown, 1959); William R. Taylor, *Cavalier and Yankee* (New York: Braziller, 1961); Edmund Wilson, *Patriotic Gore* (New York: Oxford Univ. Press, 1962).

Gentleman. A descendant of Cavaliers, the gentleman demanded two things of life—racial purity and an adherence to a strict chivalric code. The donee of his chivalry, the Southern woman, embodied all the feminine virtues. The third place in this scheme belonged to the blacks, the dancing darkies who worshiped their mistress and master, sang songs, told stories like Uncle Remus and, all in all, led a rather leisurely existence.

By the 1880's Southern writers elaborated upon the myth of the Old South and provided it with a new focal point, resulting from the experience of the Civil War and the Reconstruction years. Despite the many differences in the Reconstruction fiction of Joel Chandler Harris, Thomas Nelson Page, and Thomas Dixon, an abstract of their common narrative background reveals something like this:

> After the war there existed in the impoverished South a sense of defeat yet a hope for the future. Southerners wanted to patch up the old wounds and to try never to be poor again, that is to say, to rebuild the Old South. The Yankees, however, would not be content with their Pyrrhic victory; with the death of Lincoln, radical Northerners, descendants of Republicans and rabid abolitionists, took control of Congress and succeeded in imposing upon the South, among other things, black rule and greater poverty. In the end, only time, the removal of the radical elements in Congress, and the deeds of the Klan prevented total disaster. Many Northerners married daughters of the Old South and thereby brought reconciliation of a deeper sort. Finally the scalawags and carpetbaggers left, the misled black man was put in place, and to the relief of good black and white folk, civilization was saved. But the legacy of Reconstruction remains, for the New South, though it preserves the moral and social codes of the old regime, never again was able to achieve the grandeur of the Old South.

Here we find the concomitant to the legend of the Old South, an elaborate postscript which adds clarity and depth to the older story. Whatever the realities of postwar life in the South, Reconstruction became for Southern writers a necessary adjunct to their concept of the antebellum South. And though time diminished the initial impact of *Uncle Tom's Cabin,* Reconstruction novelists shaped their materials around the characters and issues that Mrs. Stowe had established nearly a generation before.

Mrs. Stowe's desire for the enlightened unity of all sections of the nation paralleled the tone sought by many Southerners in the late nineteenth century. In the 1880's Henry W. Grady's "New South" program supported emerging middle-class interests and influenced the thinking of writers like Thomas Nelson Page and Joel Chandler Harris. In their view, the South could get back into the mainstream of American life only by convincing Northern industrial interests of the region's progressive goals and of its lack of internal strife—particularly racial strife.[6] Consequently, Southern Re-

[6] Paul M. Gaston, *The New South Creed* (New York: Knopf, 1970), passim.

construction fiction attempted to justify the ways of the South to Northern man—which helps account for the theme of reconciliation that permeates these books. Page's novels and stories represent the genre at its apogee. In *Red Rock* (1898) the patching up of old wounds is obvious and, in its way, seductive. Realizing, as one of the characters observes, "There was no Mason and Dixon line in love," Page has a set of mixed (Northern and Southern) marriages take place.[7] There are also a series of North-South friendships like that of Dr. Cary and Senator Rockfield; and Northerners speak profusely of the grandeur of the South's customs and its landscape. Though the antebellum novels of William Alexander Caruthers, John Esten Cooke, and John Pendleton Kennedy avoided all but a superficial glimpse at the slave's life, Page's *Red Rock* and his short fiction resurrected and elaborated upon the Old South's "Uncle Tom"—an "Uncle Tom" shorn of the depth and human dignity that Mrs. Stowe tried to give her character. The smiling black lackey holding the plantation owner's stirrups in a novel by Caruthers or Cooke found a voice in Page's fiction, and in stories like "Marse Chan" and "Meh Lady" he spoke nostalgically of his old master and mistress and of the happy times "befo' da wah."

In *Red Rock,* alongside the good ex-slave who yearns for the glory of the Old South's master-slave relationship, Page includes a philosophic repudiation of slavery as an institution. Southerners like Page realized that, though with emancipation slavery died as an institution, the abolitionist's view of the South's treatment of blacks—of which Mrs. Stowe's was the best known—remained embedded in the national memory. And the voice of Southerners like George W. Cable provided a public reminder that the "Negro Question" remained unresolved in the South.[8] Therefore, with Mrs. Stowe's Legree in the background, Page set about to absolve the old Southern plantation owner by shifting the burden of slavery's cruelty to the overseer, a ploy that depended on a growing popular misconception of Legree as an overseer, not the plantation owner Mrs. Stowe made him. All of this was not accidental for, as Jay B. Hubbell has written, *Red Rock* "was in effect a belated reply to *Uncle Tom's Cabin.*"[9]

Joel Chandler Harris wrote editorials for Grady's Atlanta *Constitution,* and like Grady supported the New South's image of a lasting affection between the races that grew out of the antebellum days.[10] Harris's early contact with black plantation life combined with the New South's ideology

[7]Thomas Nelson Page, *Red Rock* (New York: Scribner's, 1898), 41.
[8]Cf. George W. Cable, *The Negro Question,* ed. Arlin Turner (New York: Doubleday, 1958), passim.
[9]Jay B. Hubbell, *The South in American Literature: 1607-1900* (Durham: Duke Univ. Press, 1954), 801.
[10]Cf. Julia C. Harris, *Joel Chandler Harris, Editor and Essayist* (Chapel Hill: Univ. of North Carolina Press, 1931), 98-104.

to produce the first major black figure in American literature since Uncle Tom. With the character of Uncle Remus, Harris succeeded more fully than Page in impressing upon the national consciousness a portrait of a "reconstructed" Uncle Tom. In his introduction to the Uncle Remus stories (1880), Harris stated explicitly what Page only implied: the shadow of Mrs. Stowe provided the shaping force behind their portraits of black life in the South.

> I trust I have been successful in presenting [in the character of Uncle Remus] what must be, at least to a large portion of American readers, a new and by no means unattractive phase of negro character—a phase which may be considered a curiously sympathetic supplement to Mrs. Stowe's wonderful defense of slavery as it existed in the South. Mrs. Stowe, let me hasten to say, attacked the possibilities of slavery with all the eloquence of genius; but the same genius painted the portrait of the Southern slaveowner, and defended him.[11]

Like Uncle Tom, Uncle Remus projects a paternalistic conception of the "negro character," but Harris manipulates the image so that it serves as an apologia for the South. The perverse assertion of Mrs. Stowe's "wonderful defense of slavery" reached a large (and young) audience before her death, and Harris, like Page, glorified a castrated Uncle Tom. Moreover, the history of Legree's transmogrification into the overseer-villain—for which the Tom plays usually get the credit—forgets the role of writers like Page and Harris in the process. Both writers simplify Mrs. Stowe's more complex portraits of the Shelbys and St. Clare. In Uncle Remus's stories, for example, all antebellum brutality toward slaves is attributed to anonymous overseers, not the masters. In this literature, then, Uncle Remus becomes Uncle Tom, the overseer becomes Legree, and Shelby and St. Clare become the Southern slaveowners whom Mrs. Stowe "defended."

* * *

However garbled *Uncle Tom's Cabin* became in the hands of Page and Harris, they generally followed W. G. Simms's earlier example and attacked Mrs. Stowe only indirectly.[12] But Thomas Dixon—remembered today mainly for his novel *The Clansman,* which served as the basis for D. W. Griffith's film "Birth of a Nation"—achieved a more complete and direct metamorphosis of *Uncle Tom.* In 1900 Dixon began writing a trilogy of Reconstruction novels, but the tenor and vehemence of his relationship to

---

[11] Joel Chandler Harris, *Uncle Remus: His Songs and His Sayings* (New York: Appleton-Century, 1937), viii.

[12] Cf. Joseph V. Ridgely, "*Woodcraft:* Simms's First Answer to Uncle Tom's Cabin," *American Literature,* 31 (January 1960), 421-33.

Mrs. Stowe place him squarely in the line of anti-Tom novels and plays produced in the South after *Uncle Tom's* publication. In his version of Southern history and of the racial question, Dixon represents a conservative reaction to the relatively benign (if paternalistic) politics of the New South group, and as such he became a self-appointed spokesman for the South at the opening of the new century.

Dixon began his career as a novelist after trying his hand at acting, at serving as a state legislator in his native North Carolina, and at the ministry, where his eloquence and progressive politics brought him to pulpits in Boston and New York as well as in the South. He conceived his first book, *The Leopard's Spots* (1902), as part of a trilogy which finally included *The Clansman* (1905) and *The Traitor* (1907). Henryk Sienkiewicz's trilogy of historical novels on Poland provided the form and theme for Dixon's saga of a suffering homeland, but *Uncle Tom's Cabin* offered a text, a set of characters, and the major challenge for *The Leopard's Spots.* Dixon himself traced the origins of his writing career to a theatrical performance of *Uncle Tom's Cabin.* Angered by what he considered the play's unjust treatment of the South, he left the theater vowing to tell the South's "true story."[13] Dixon first considered calling *The Leopard's Spots* "The Rise of Simon Legree," a title which suggests that as initially conceived the focus of the narrative followed the established line of the overseer-villain Legree. The final product, however, resulted in a more thoroughgoing revision of *Uncle Tom's Cabin.*

The Leopard's Spots rivalled the publishing sensation of Uncle Tom. An immediate success, it sold over a million copies and helped to establish Doubleday, Page as a major publishing house. Translated into a dozen languages, the book gained Dixon an international reputation. Reviewers chided Dixon for his racism, but many reflected the opinion expressed in Max Nordau's letter to him: "*The Leopard's Spots* is the most powerful novel I have read for years. . . . Man! Are you conscious of your immense responsibility? You have deliberately undone the work of Harriet Beecher Stowe."[14] Dixon was only too aware of his relation to Mrs. Stowe:

> "I claim the book is an authentic human document and I know it is the most important moral deed of my life. It may shock the prejudice of those who have idealized or worshipped the negro as canonized in 'Uncle Tom.' Is it not time they heard the whole truth? They have heard only one side for forty years."[15]

It is a tribute to *Uncle Tom's Cabin*—and an insight into its hold upon

[13]Raymond Allen Cook, *Fire from the Flint: The Amazing Careers of Thomas Dixon* (Winston-Salem: J. F. Blair, 1968), 105.

[14]Quoted in Cook, 114.

[15]In E. F. Harkins, *Little Pilgrimages Among the Men Who Have Written Famous Books,* 2d ser. (Boston: Page, 1903), 121.

American thought—that Mrs. Stowe's book still elicited a full-scale "answer" after forty years. This time the reply was not a mere local effusion but a book that reached an audience comparable to Mrs. Stowe's.

The subtitle of *The Leopard's Spots,* "A Romance of the White Man's Burden (1865-1900)," indicates the course of the argument for the "other side." The narrative deals not only with a regional problem but with an obstacle facing all white men, in particular America's Anglo-Saxons. Consequently, Dixon was able to jettison the Old South and to use it merely as a convenient reference point from which to gauge the damage inflicted by Reconstruction. The action of the novel extends, significantly, from the end of the war to the turn of the century, thus providing its readers with both a historical and a contemporary setting. "Book I" ("Legree's Regime") offers the same bleak picture of Reconstruction found in *Red Rock,* with scalawags and carpetbaggers, freed blacks and the Freedmen's Bureau making life miserable for war-torn Southerners. The trappings are the same, but there are a few important innovations.

First of all, Dixon introduces a new version of the former slave. Page's blacks tended to be either pickanniny types—docile, funloving caricatures— or the faithful servants of benevolent masters. Emancipation produces what we expect from such creatures: petty thefts, drunkenness, and personal chaos in the face of independence. There are, to be sure, instances of the renegade, and once in *Red Rock* a band of blacks *almost* manhandles a white woman before a vigilance committee steps in. With Dixon the order is reversed. Like Page—and Harris in his Reconstruction novel, *Gabriel Tolliver* (1902)—Dixon blames Republican rule for black misconduct; but the fact remains that his version of the Afro-American is bestial. Dixon's black man shows the effect of the pervasive racial Darwinism of the period:[16] he is a genetically inferior, oversexed animal whose minute intelligence directs itself toward one goal—the wives and daughters of the white man. A black leader in *The Leopard's Spots,* Tim Shelby (formerly attached to Mrs. Stowe's Shelbys of Kentucky), speaks of his new place in a reconstructed South:

> Our proud white aristocrats of the South are in a panic, it seems. They feel the coming power of the Negro. They fear their Desdemonas may be fascinated by an Othello! Well, Othello's day has come at last. . . . I expect to lead a white bride into my house before another year and have poor white aristocrats to tend my lawn.[17]

[16]Cf. Richard Hofstadter, *Social Darwinism in American Thought* (1944; rpt. Boston: Beacon, 1965), 170-200.

[17]Thomas Dixon, *The Leopard's Spots: A Romance of the White Man's Burden—1865-1900* (New York: Grosset & Dunlap, 1902), 90. All subsequent citations of *The Leopard's Spots* are from this edition.

Such is Dixon's archetypal black: a former slave deceptively bearing Mrs. Stowe's imprimatur who attacks white culture where it most hurts—in its pocketbook and in its women's virtue. Dixon translates Mrs. Stowe's earlier uncertainties over the possible destiny of the slave's descendants in America into a picture of racial confrontation that she would not have understood. The black man, in effect, not only seizes political control but comes close to reversing his historical role. Whereas in Mrs. Stowe's view, the white man had indefensible chattel rights over his slaves, in Dixon it is the black man who threatens to possess the white woman and to harness the white man as a labor force.

Two other figures from *Uncle Tom* implement this program: Mrs. Stowe's vicious slave-trader, Dave Haley, proves even more vicious as Shelby's cohort; and Simon Legree completes the triangle. Dixon resurrects Legree, and although a sorry silhouette of that tortured, malignant man who abused Uncle Tom, he serves his purpose as a symbol for "everything that the soul of the South loathes" (196). Though his hands are "red with the blood of their race" (164), Legree succeeds in marshaling blacks into a formidable state government. As Speaker of the House he introduces a bill which dissolves the marital bonds of all citizens who fought against the Union—presumably so that his black underlings might then be free to intermarry with "white aristocrats." Dixon, in effect, takes over Mrs. Stowe's theme of the sanctity of motherhood and of family life, and, in an inversion of her thesis, assigns Legree his old function as violator of the home. *Uncle Tom's* familial rhetoric originally served to undermine the false paternal self-image with which slave owners justified the destruction of their chattels' family life. Dixon borrows Mrs. Stowe's terms and exploits them to undo her point about the strength of black familial ties and to condone the actions of the very class against whom they were originally aimed.

Legree's campaign to destroy white family bonds also provides Dixon with a historical justification for the rise and deeds of the Klan. The Clansmen depose Legree and he flees to the North, leaving behind a terrible legacy: "[As a result of his reign] the younger generation of white men only knew the negro as an enemy of his people in politics and society" (404). Dixon thus probes the basis of the South's defense of its plantation owners, as he ascribes the roots of Southern racial violence to the misdeeds of Mrs. Stowe's Northern "overseer." The logic of this maneuver stems from Mrs. Stowe's keen awareness of the extent to which both North and South shared in the guilt of slavery.

... the sons of the free states ... are the holders, and, proverbially, the hardest masters of slaves; the sons of the free states ... have connived at the extension of slavery, in our national body; the sons of the free states ... trade the souls and bodies of men as an equivalent to money, in their mercantile dealings. There are multitudes of slaves temporarily owned, and sold again, by merchants in northern cities; and shall the whole guilt or obloquy of slavery fall only on the South?[18]

Mrs. Stowe's decision to make the novel's archvillain a nightmare version of the Yankee peddler dramatized this point, as it also highlighted the capitalist basis of slavery. In turn Dixon puts this dimension of Legree's character to other uses, as he concludes the ex-overseer-Reconstruction leader's Southern literary career and sends him home to New England.

Twenty-five years after Reconstruction we again encounter Legree, and the changes he underwent show Dixon's grasp of Mrs. Stowe's character: the "new Legree" of 1900 is a diamond-studded, well-spoken (he went to finishing school!) capitalist who exploits the white working class. Legree the tycoon is the owner of Northern mills and factories, and he profits from a system whose abuses led to the period's labor reforms and to the rise of unionized labor, both of which Dixon portrays sympathetically in the novel. Dixon invites a comparison between the fashionable Legree and Mrs. Stowe's character.

> ... the picture of that brute with a whip in his hand beating a negro caused the most terrible war in the history of the world. Three millions of men flew at each other's throats and for four years fought like demons.... He was a poor harmless fool there beating his own faithful slave to death. Compare that Legree with the one today, and you compare a mere stupid man with a prince of hell. (405)

Legree's former black concubines were limited to Cassy and a few mulatto house slaves; now "it is said he has murdered the souls of many innocent [white] girls in these mills" (404). Dixon's argument again echoes an older line of defense: George Fitzhugh, one of the most persuasive proslavery apologists of the 1850's, had argued that blacks under slavery were less savagely used than the working class of industrialized nations.[19]

Southern slavery, Dixon implies, was relatively beneficent compared to the industrial wage system of the urban North. The contrast between the evils of a commercial North and a mellower South runs deep in Southern literature, from the novels of John Pendleton Kennedy to the agrarian essays in *I'll Take My Stand*. Though Mrs. Stowe drew many elements from this tradition, it is to her credit that she resisted this particular stereotype. She believed that the economic system of the South, however agrarian in nature, was based firmly on capitalist motives. St. Clare unmistakably speaks for Mrs. Stowe when he argues:

---

[18]Harriet Beecher Stowe, *Uncle Tom's Cabin, or Life Among the Lowly* (New York: Modern Library, 1948), 546. All subsequent citations of *Uncle Tom* are from this edition.

[19]George Fitzhugh, *Sociology for the South* (Richmond: Morris, 1854), passim.

... the American planter is only doing, in another form, what the English aristocracy and capitalists are doing by the lower classes; that is, I take it, *appropriating* them, body and bone, soul and spirit, to their use and convenience. . . . The slave owner can whip his refractory slave to death,—the capitalist can starve him to death. (284)

In the slave-holding South, then, Legree's native instincts find natural outlets. When Dixon took over the character, he put Legree's Yankee traits to more familiar uses. Dixon's urban experience as a minister in Boston and New York made him aware of a type of industrial slavery that was both comparable to Southern slavery and a more pressing issue at the turn of the century. In projecting the logical course of Legree's career in the North, Dixon reinstated him as the national villain by depicting him as an industrial lord who profited from transporting blacks to a North which was having trouble feeding itself.

Dixon's version of Legree's career helps account for *The Leopard's Spots'* remarkable popularity. His character suited the times, in much the same way that Mrs. Stowe's Legree suited the 1850's. The turn of the century, after all, saw a great migration of Southern blacks to Northern cities—an event which, taken together with the continuing influx of European immigrants, posed a new economic and social threat to the North. The migrations produced a strong backlash of nativist racial sentiment that affected both groups.[20] As blacks were trekking North, a mass of immigrants was streaming in from Europe, and for the first time many Northerners began to assume that what they were saying—what they feared— about the immigrants was precisely what the Southern white had been saying all along about the black man. George M. Frederickson has described the North's situation at this time:

The race question had always been a national one. . . . But for many Northerners the problem of black-white relations had often seemed less critical than other social issues simply because most blacks were in the South. As this situation changed . . . it became clear that the North had a very serious race problem of its own stemming from the forced ghettoization of masses of blacks in its cities.[21]

Between 1900 and 1904 living conditions and economic conflicts caused Northern antiblack riots in urban centers from New York to Springfield, Ohio. John Hope Franklin surmises that this ". . . rioting in the North was as vicious and almost as prevalent as in the South."[22] In this atmosphere, Dixon's portrayal of Legree as a Northern industrialist who manipulates

[20]Cf. John Higham, *Strangers in the Land: Patterns of American Nativism, 1860-1925* (1955; rpt. New York: Atheneum, 1973), 131-57.
[21]Frederickson, *The Black Image,* 325.
[22]John Hope Franklin, *From Slavery to Freedom: A History of Negro Americans* (1947; rpt. New York: Knopf, 1969), 439.

black labor for his own ends struck a chord in the public imagination. Dixon's Legree not only obscured Mrs. Stowe's argument but effected an implicit vindication of Southern (and Northern) racial violence.

Legree served another and related function in Dixon's novel. Just as Mrs. Stowe created the character to dramatize the cruelty perpetrated among the "lowly" by vested interests, so Dixon used Legree to play on both conservative and progressive apprehensions over the plight of the new lowly— the "poor whites" in both North and South, one of whose chief claims to social status, incidentally, was their white skin. Intead of uniting with blacks in an offensive against the sources of their common oppression—the industrial complex of the North, the merchants and large landlords of the South—poor whites in both regions tended to identify their distress with black and immigrant labor.[23] Dixon never shows Legree's effect on an individual Northern laborer; references are made always to the *mass* of poor white workers that suffer under his rule. But there is one character—a Southern poor white—whom Dixon has Legree torture in much the same way he did Uncle Tom.

In Dixon's novel the character of Tom Camp emerges as the archetypal poor white Southerner. Tom Camp competes in Dixon's imagination with the book's proclaimed hero, Charles Gaston, who acts in the best tradition of the Old South's "aristocracy" and wins the "lady" and the governor's mansion by the time the book ends. Beside such an obvious hero, Dixon places his idealized version of the poor white, representing the class in some ways most affected by the enfranchisement of the black Southerner. Through this figure Dixon achieves his most audacious transformation of *Uncle Tom's Cabin,* as he reconstructs Uncle Tom in the character of Tom Camp.

Dixon introduces Tom Camp as a former Confederate soldier whose part in the war cost him a leg; he returns home to find himself poorer than when he left. Structurally, Tom Camp's role in the novel corresponds to Uncle Tom's in Mrs. Stowe's book. Tom Camp lives in a cabin in the shadow of one of the big Southern houses; like Uncle Tom his dialect reflects his lower-class status; and he also refuses to share in the traditional hatred of his group for the ruling class. He serves, too, as a humble spiritual model for white aristocrats: patience and faith are his virtues, and he is as devoted a Bible-quoting Christian as Uncle Tom. His Christian strength makes him something of an oracle in the community. The only difference between Tom Camp and Uncle Tom is that the saintly Camp can hate one living

---

[23]Cf. Robert L. Allen, *Reluctant Reformers: Racism and Social Reform Movements in the United States* (Washington, D.C.: Howard Univ. Press, 1974), 49–79. Allen discusses the failure of the Populist movement of this period in terms of the racial antagonism between poor whites and the poor blacks.

creature—the black man:

> My daddy an my mommy hated 'em before me somehow, we always felt like they
> was crowdin' us to death on them big plantations and the little ones too. . . . (28)

Although Camp is a Southerner reflecting on an agrarian past, it takes very little of this sort of thing to see that Dixon is appealing to both Northern and Southern fears of social displacement.

Dixon makes Tom Camp's hatred appear natural since, again like Uncle Tom, the poor white faces the loss of his home and his children at the hands of Simon Legree and his black assistants. When the liberated blacks rape and kill one of his daughters, Tom Camp experiences his one crisis of faith. Dixon studied *Uncle Tom's Cabin* with more care than many later critics of the book who forget chapters XXXIII and XXXIV and accuse Uncle Tom of a too easy Christian faith. Dixon models Tom Camp's struggle to retain his faith on the sustained temptation to atheism that Mrs. Stowe's Tom undergoes in those chapters. Dixon's character also passes through the shadows and emerges as a pious martyr; in the end Tom Camp dies under the strain, sacrificed as was Uncle Tom. Clearly, Dixon envisioned a new suffering Christ image for America. In this respect, he went beyond the reconstructed Uncle Toms of Page and Harris. They had simply nudged Mrs. Stowe's Tom gently into the Southern fold as Uncle Remus, that is, as a black man who suffered none of the *angst* of Uncle Tom. But Dixon displaced the pious ex-slave, and by adhering more closely to Mrs. Stowe's model, he created a white Uncle Tom, a poor white crucified both psychologically and economically by the black man under the tutelage of an industrialized Simon Legree. It is an image to which many, North and South, responded—and still do.

* * *

Mrs. Stowe ended her book on a self-consciously prophetic note. Her vision of black history in America included exportation to a free colony in Liberia—a solution that she has George Harris and his family embrace. As Cushing Strout has remarked, "It is in [Mrs. Stowe's] policy of exporting free negroes, which Lincoln also accepted, that she betrays a moral evasion of the deeper dilemmas inherent in the history of American race relations."[24] Mrs. Stowe's advocacy of African colonization for American blacks reflects the racial ambivalence inherent in the reform movements

[24] Strout, "*Uncle Tom's Cabin* and the Portent of Millenium," 383.

from which she drew many of her ideas.[25] From her deeply Christian point of view, she justified colonization as an analogue to the biblical Exodus.[26]

> When an enlightened and Christianized community shall have, on the shores of Africa, laws, language and literature, drawn from among us, may then the scenes of the house of bondage be to them like the remembrance of Egypt to the Israelites,—a motive of thankfulness to Him who hath redeemed them! (xxii)

Yet the fact remains that however sympathetic to black Americans, however outraged at their inhumane treatment under slavery, Mrs. Stowe shared what one historian calls "the tragic limitation of the white racial imagination of the nineteenth century, namely its characteristic inability to visualize an egalitarian biracial society."[27]

Though Mrs. Stowe did not espouse an unequivocal theory of black inferiority—in fact, she tended to propose black superiority in areas such as natural piety and Christian virtuousness[28]—her stance clearly lends itself to arguments for black inferiority. (*Uncle Tom,* after all, is spotted with references to black racial characteristics that Mrs. Stowe thought of as exhibiting "the highest form of the peculiarly *Christian life*": "their [the black's] gentleness, their lowly docility of heart, their aptitude to repose on a superior mind and rest on a higher power, their childlike simplicity of affection, and facility of forgiveness" [223].) Dixon's book is a significant example of the dangers of Mrs. Stowe's position. Her exclusion of blacks from a viable political and social role in American life—however well-intentioned—reaps its bitter harvest in Dixon's vision of "The New America" of 1900 in *The Leopard's Spots.*

Also advocating exportation, Dixon dramatizes Mrs. Stowe's anxiety

[25]Cf. Allen, *Reluctant Reformers,* 11–48; and Frederickson, 1–42, 97–129.

[26]In this respect, Mrs. Stowe broke with the more radical abolitionists who insisted on the black man's equality and his right to an equal place in American society. For example, see William Lloyd Garrison's review of *Uncle Tom* in *The Liberator,* 22 (March 26, 1852). Garrison said that the story brought tears to his eyes and that it would "awaken the strongest compassion for the oppressed and the utmost abhorrence of the system which grinds them to dust." Yet his one objection to the book was that "towards its conclusion, [it] contains some objectionable sentiments respecting African colonization."

[27]Frederickson, xii. Frederickson sees Mrs. Stowe as sharing the "romantic racialism" of much nineteenth century antislavery thought. According to him, "Although romantic racialists acknowledged that blacks were different from whites and probably always would be, they projected an image of the negro that could be construed as flattering or laudatory in the context of some currently accepted ideals of human behavior and sensibility" (101–02). Frederickson suggests that the romantic racialists were generally "benevolent in intent" (125) and that "their time and place provided them neither the means nor the social philosophy to deal adequately with the ravages of racial prejudice and the growth of racism as an ideology" (42).

[28]Charles Dickens, in fact, felt Mrs. Stowe had gone too far in this respect. In a letter to her, he congratulated her on her book, saying he enjoyed it but that he thought the fault of the book was that it makes the "African race to be a great race." Quoted in Catherine Gilbertson, *Harriet Beecher Stowe* (New York: Appleton-Century, 1937), 160.

over the descendants of freed slaves in America by depicting the plight of
George and Eliza Harris' son in the America of 1900. He gives the Harris
boy, named "Little Harry" by Mrs. Stowe, the fine education she projected
for him; Dixon renames him George, Jr., and makes him a Harvard
graduate. George Harris' experience instructs us that when a black man,
however well-bred, attempts to court a white woman in 1900, he is a
revolting object to the lady's parent, even though the parent is a Northern
civil rights leader—in this case the liberal Senator Lowell of Massachusetts.
Dixon understood the latent racism, particularly over the question of
biracial marriage, that often accompanied the most devoted antislavery ad-
vocates.[29] Previous to the marriage proposal, Lowell—whose family tree includes a few abolitionists—had found in George Harris a brilliant protégé.
Inverting the pattern of reversals that Mrs. Stowe used so effectively in
chapters such as "In Which it Appears that a Senator is but a Man," Dixon
uses Senator Lowell's rejection of Harris to define the failure of black
experience in America by exploring the limits of what W. E. B. DuBois
called, one year after the publication of *The Leopard's Spots,* the "color-
line."[30]

The novel ends with a disillusioned George Harris leaving Harvard and
subsequently being hindered by powerful unions from finding even menial
work in industry. Hugh Halliday, the son of the Quakers who helped
George's parents to escape in *Uncle Tom,* appears as a union leader; but unlike his parents Halliday finds himself powerless to help in "the New
America." Economic exclusion forces Harris into a life of crime, and in his
travels about the country he discovers the symbols of the new era:

> [He visited] the scenes in Colorado, Kansas, Indiana, and Ohio, where Negroes
> had recently been burned alive. He would find the ash-heap and place on it a
> wreath of costly flowers. He lingered thoughtfully over the ash-pits he found in
> Kansas made from the flesh of living Negroes. He tried to imagine the figure of
> John Brown marching by his side, but instead he felt the grip of Simon Legree's
> hand on his throat, living, militant, omnipotent. His soul had conquered the
> world. Yet even Legree had never dared to burn a Negro to death in the old days
> of slavery. . . . He went to the spot where his mother had climbed up the banks of
> the Ohio River into the promised land of liberty, and followed the track of the old
> underground Railroad for fugitive slaves a few miles. He came to a village which
> was once a station of this system. Here, strangest of all, he found one of these ash-
> heaps in the public square. (407)

Ironically, one of the few moving moments in *The Leopard's Spots* is this
scene in which the curtain is dramatically lowered on a book that typified an

---

[29]Cf. Allen, *Reluctant Reformers,* 29–39.
[30]W. E. B. DuBois, *The Souls of Black Folk* (Chicago: McClurg, 1903), 13.

era; wreaths and the remains of lynch fires mark those scenes that Mrs. Stowe had made the emblems of freedom for a generation. Replacing Mrs. Stowe's language of evangelical humanism with an equally fervent rhetoric of white manifest destiny, Dixon projects a vision of a "New America" in which rich and poor, North and South, foreign-born and native are united in a new bond. There remains only one Ishmael in this new covenant.

Anticipating Richard Wright by a generation, George Harris' story, if written in outrage, would be no anomaly in *Uncle Tom's Children*. Dixon's book poses the problem of how direct a progeny of Mrs. Stowe are Wright's children—and indeed all our Uncle Toms and their children. The example of Page, Harris, and Dixon suggests that to understand Mrs. Stowe's relationship to our own Uncle Toms we would do well to look beyond the Tom plays and beyond our own myopic view of *Uncle Tom's Cabin*.

CONSTANCE ROURKE IN CONTEXT: THE USES OF MYTH

JOAN SHELLEY RUBIN
McMaster University

BETWEEN 1915 AND 1941, CONSTANCE ROURKE PRODUCED SIX BOOKS, OVER one hundred articles and reviews, and a massive number of notes and drafts for a projected three-volume "History of American Culture." Her best-known work, *American Humor* (1931), continues to draw attention, especially from literary critics debating the connections she made between folklore and the achievements of our greatest writers. Yet the recognition of Rourke's true importance is fading. Her significance lies not in any of her particular critical discussions, but in the major themes which mark all her work, biography and history as well as literary analysis. The emphasis on Rourke as literary critic has impeded the historian's exploration of those themes and their origins. Like the obscure folk tales she brought to light, the context for Rourke's writing now requires excavation. An examination of the intellectual and emotional sources for the most prominent of Rourke's recurrent concepts—the idea of myth—provides a new understanding of all her work, according it a historical value which transcends her literary judgments.

The word "myth" permeates Rourke's writing to such an extent that the term loses precise meaning. Throughout *American Humor,* for example, Rourke used "myth" interchangeably with "legend" and "fantasy," as in her descriptions of the Yankee peddler. "A barrier seemed to lie between this legendary Yankee and any effort to reach his inner character . . . ," Rourke wrote. "He was consistently a mythical figure. . . . Plain and pawky, he was an ideal image."[1] Along the same lines, she noted: "He was a myth, a fantasy. Many hands had joined to fashion his figure, from the South, from the West, even from New England. What the Yankee peddler was in life and fact can only be guessed."[2] Rourke's repeated failure to draw

---

[1] Constance Rourke, *American Humor: A Study of the National Character* (New York: Harcourt, Brace, 1931), 30. Hereafter cited as *AH.*
[2] *AH,* 5.

distinctions among myth, fantasy, and legend, and elsewhere between fable
and epic, cumulatively establishes her fundamental thesis about the
American character—that, as she put it in the opening sentence of an
unpublished essay on American theatricals, "We are a nation of myth
makers."[3] Other instances of the numerous references to myth in *American
Humor* include the description of early minstrelsy as "woven deep" with
"Western myth-making,"[4] the claim that "popular declamation of the
[18]30's and [18]40's has often been considered as bombast when it should be
taken as comic mythology,"[5] the discussion of the role of Indian myths in
burlesque,[6] and the use of the phrase "the accumulated American myth."[7]

Rourke saw her demonstration of the American propensity for myth as a
central argument of *American Humor,* and one of that work's contributions
to scholarship. In a heated exchange with the historian and critic Bernard
DeVoto, she objected to DeVoto's proposed discussion of her book in his
Mark Twain's America, asserting: "I feel that the outlining of the element
of fantasy in American humor is something specially my own. So far as I
know this has not been done before. . . . I believe that even the use of the
word 'fantasy' in relation to American humor is entirely my own."[8] On the
contrary, DeVoto insisted that frontier humor entailed the "realistic portrayal of character," without exhibiting what Rourke called the "transition
into fantasy." DeVoto had planned a footnote refuting Rourke, based on his
reading of newspapers of the Southwest: "There were a vast number of
characteristic themes but I cannot see that the individual treatments of
them are anti-realistic. . . . In my opinion, an overwhelming weight of evidence contradicts Miss Rourke's thesis."[9] The dispute between Rourke and
DeVoto is a sign that the concept of the American as myth-maker was not
self-evident but instead required concerted proof.

Apart from *American Humor,* Rourke's attempt to amass such proof led
her in several instances to offer novel interpretations of historical documents. For example, her unpublished "History of American Culture," the
manuscript on which she was working at the time of her death, treats
Hakluyt's *Voyages* and the early maps of explorers as fantasies about the
unknown continent. Subsequent discussions in the notes for "American Culture" extend the myth-making tendencies Rourke detected in America's
earliest stages to such diverse efforts as the writings of Washington Irving,

[3]"Old American Theatricals," Constance Rourke Papers. Hereafter cited as CR Papers.
[4]*AH,* 91.
[5]*AH,* 64.
[6]*AH,* 131.
[7]*AH,* 141.
[8]Rourke to DeVoto, March 3, 1932, CR Papers.
[9]DeVoto to Rourke, Dec. 17, 1931, CR Papers.

Mark Twain, and Henry Adams, as well as to folk art and the landscape painting of the Hudson River School.

Rourke's attraction to myth underlies her biographical studies as well, and goes a long way toward rescuing certain of those studies from critical disfavor. As Rourke treated them, the Beechers, Horace Greeley, and P. T. Barnum gripped the public imagination and became subjects for legend (*Trumpets of Jubilee,* 1927); Lola Montez, the California Gold Rush actress, was conceivably Byron's daughter (*Troupers of the Gold Coast,* 1928); David Crockett carried "sunrise in his pocket" (*Davy Crockett,* 1934); and Audubon's mysterious origins made him possibly the lost French Dauphin (*Audubon,* 1936). When Stanley Hyman judged Rourke's attention to the Dauphin legend a mark of her "gullibility" and disparaged *Davy Crockett* for its unrealistic mixture of "tall talk" and historical data, he ignored her basic intention: not to supply strict narrative but to display as much as she could of the American's effort to create characters of mythical proportions.[10]

Rourke's deliberate, persistent emphasis on myth-making suggests that she used the idea of myth as a strategy to attain some intellectual goals or emotional satisfactions. At first glance, the explanation for Rourke's attention to myth seems simple enough. She knew that her evidence directly challenged Van Wyck Brooks' laments in *The Wine of the Puritans* (1908) and *Letters and Leadership* (1918) that "we have no myths"[11] and no "national fabric of spiritual experience."[12] In 1918, when Brooks had demanded a "usable past" to nourish future generations of artists, Rourke, who first knew Brooks in her capacity as contributor to his *Dial* and *Freeman,* had answered his call. Yet while Rourke shared Brooks' conception of the "organic" connection between rich traditions and great art, she adopted only the first half of his instruction to "Discover, invent a usable past." Rourke's detection of native myths placed her in an adversary relationship to Brooks. Her books are all works of advocacy in a debate with Brooks and his supporters about America's artistic resources, a debate which explains the defensive quality just below the surface of *American Humor* and which accounts for the terms in which she described what she called "the national character." In contrast to Brooks' (and other intellectuals') portrait of American life as sterile, materialistic, devoid of fantasy, and fragmented into "high-brow" and "low-brow" elements which paralyzed the creative

[10]Stanley Hyman, *The Armed Vision* (New York: Knopf, 1948), 130.

[11]Van Wyck Brooks, "The Wine of the Puritans," in Claire Sprague, ed., *Van Wyck Brooks: The Early Years* (New York: Harper Torchbooks, 1968), 37.

[12]Van Wyck Brooks, "Letters and Leadership," in *Three Essays on America* (New York: Dutton, 1934), 134.

artist, Rourke depicted an America unified by an interest in that spiritual activity, myth-making.

Rourke was convincing. As Brooks later conceded, by the early 1930s he himself had developed new sympathies toward American culture, in part because Rourke's work had "indefinitely broadened" his "horizon."[13] But Rourke's attitude toward the American past was more ambiguous than Brooks' acknowledgment implies, and her affirmative stance at times more the result of wish than belief. Though the positive strain dominates in Rourke's writings, her work sometimes betrays the recognition that Brooks' assessment of America was correct. Along with her eager rebuttal of Brooks on the grounds that American myths had already furnished a "usable past" lay her suspicion that myth-making was only a first step in the achievement of an adequate culture—or, worse, that our myths were actually insufficient. Hence Rourke invoked myth in defense of American culture for a double purpose: both to disprove Brooks' assertions and to accommodate them.

Rourke's interpretation of theories about the nature of myth and its relationship to art reflects her desire to defend America against Brooks' charges while assuaging her own doubts. Some readers[14] have noticed the impact on Rourke of two writers on myth, Giambattista Vico and J. G. Herder, whose work she herself cited in *The Roots of American Culture* (1942), a posthumous collection of previously unpublished writings which Brooks edited. Vico's emphasis in *The New Science* (1725) on the vital relationship between popular traditions (rather than individual masterpieces) and the growth of a culture convinced Rourke of the importance of folklore to the development of art. Herder's similar idea that myth formed the basis for any national culture strengthened Rourke's belief that the fine arts required the existence of a native mythology. But it was her intellectual encounter with a later group of scholars—the so-called Cambridge School of classicists—which did most to shape Rourke's view and to inform her defense of American culture.

The Cambridge School—dominated by Sir James G. Frazer, expanded in the work of Andrew Lang, E. S. Hartland, Gilbert Murray, F. M. Cornford, and others—exerted greatest influence on Rourke through the books of Jane Ellen Harrison. Yet though Harrison is the only member of the group whose work Rourke cited directly, she was aware of several other studies along similar lines. Stanley Hyman's remark in *The Armed Vision* that Harrison was the only member of the Cambridge School "with whose work Miss

[13]Van Wyck Brooks, *Days of the Phoenix* (New York: Dutton, 1957), 104. Brooks' comments in a letter to Lewis Mumford dispute the extent of Rourke's influence, but there is no doubt that the impact of her work was considerable. See Robert E. Spiller, ed., *The Van Wyck Brooks–Lewis Mumford Letters* (New York: Dutton, 1970), 218–19.

[14]See for example Brooks' introduction to Rourke's *The Roots of American Culture* (New York: Harcourt, Brace and World, 1942) and Gene Bluestein, *The Voice of the Folk* (Amherst: Univ. of Massachusetts Press, 1972).

Rourke seems to have been familiar" (an assumption which led him to announce that she might have done better "with another background and a great deal more learning"[15]) is simply inaccurate: Rourke's library contained at least three books by Andrew Lang and ten (counting several translations) by Gilbert Murray. Nevertheless Harrison's *Ancient Art and Ritual* (1913) provides sufficient indication of the influence of the Cambridge School upon Rourke.

Harrison's purpose was to demonstrate that ritual (and the myths contrived to explain it) were, in her words, "rudimentary art." For example, Harrison argued, the drama developed out of the Greek fertility dance, or *dromenon,* once the religious faith and desire for immediate action accompanying the *dromenon* had disappeared. Two aspects of Harrison's theory held special appeal for Rourke: her depiction of myth-making as a communal enterprise and her understanding, as in Herder's view, of myth as the precursor of art. The festivals which Harrison discussed occurred on dates "of importance to the food-supply of the community, in summer, in winter, at the coming of the annual rains, or the regular rising of a river."[16] Given the social origins of ritual, and hence of all art, the artist emerges not as Brooks' isolated individual but as one who draws sanction and sustenance from the wider community.

American Humor reveals prominent traces of Harrison's ideas. Most suggestive is Rourke's explicit reference to early Greek religious rituals in her discussion of American revival meetings:

> Once again personal emotion was submerged in a coarse and crescent patterning of communal emotion; and the flight was toward legend. Around the simple outline of the divine comedy these people continually wove innumerable small new fables and beliefs. Once again, too, the movement was toward the theater. The orgiastic forest revivals with their pagan spirit and savage manifestations bore a not altogether distant resemblance to the Eleusinarian mysteries out of which the Greek drama had developed. A fantastic basic ritual was often present in later cults, such has been a prelude to the theater or the drama among primitive people. A minor religious theater could have been drawn from the celebration of almost any one of these new sects. All their modes were outward, rhapsodic, declamatory, full of song, verging upon the dance, adorned with symbolic costume. . . .[17]

This passage owes a large debt to *Ancient Art and Ritual.* Compare, for example, Rourke's emphasis on collective emotion and the social character of ritual (its "outward" quality) with Harrison's remark that "it is not [primitive man's] private and personal emotions that tend to become ritual, but those that are public, felt and expressed officially, that is, by the whole

[15]Hyman, 134.

[16]Jane Ellen Harrison, *Ancient Art and Ritual* (New York: Henry Holt, 1913), 74.

[17]*AH,* 135–36. See also 36–37, 54.

tribe or community."[18] Rourke's focus upon the primitive or pagan element in revival meetings—and in this passage her reference to Greek drama—reflect a desire to discover an American counterpart of Greek cultural forms. Similarly, many elements of Harrison's characterization of Greek dances invade Rourke's discussion of black minstrelsy: the stress on ritual as communal activity, the notion of the redirection of individual emotion, the interest in the minstrel performance as primitive or ritualistic. For example, she traces the "walkaround," the climactic dance of the minstrel show, back to "the communal dancing of the African."[19] A passage which concludes by arguing for the legendary quality attending the Negro character in minstrelsy—his emergence as a "type" rather than a closely delineated individual—begins:

> Primitive elements were roughly patterned in minstrelsy. Its songs, its dances, its patter, were soon set within a ritual which grew more and more fixed, like some rude ceremonial. Endmen and interlocutors spun out their talk with an air of improvisation, but this free talk and song occupied an inalienable place in the procedure. In the dancing a strong individualism appeared, and the single dancer might step out of the whole pattern; the jig dancer might perform his feats on a peck measure, and dancers might be matched against each other with high careerings which belonged to each alone; but these excursions were caught within the broad effect. Beneath them all ran the deep insurgence of Negro choruses that flowed into minstrelsy for many years, even after its ritual grew stereotyped and other elements were added; and the choral dancing of the walkaround made a resonant primitive groundwork.
>
> Within this ritualistic design certain Negro characters were permanently limned. . . . [Jim Crow, Zip Coon, Dan Tucker] all revealed the Negro character: yet they showed that greater outline and more abstract drawing which reveals the world of legend.[20]

When this passage is set against a section of *Ancient Art and Ritual* concerning the process by which actual persons become the basis for abstract personification, Rourke's affinity with Harrison becomes clear:

> . . . from many actual men and women decked with leaves, or trees dressed up as men and women, arises *the* Tree Spirit, *the* Vegetation Spirit, *the* Death.
>
> At the back, then, of the fact of personification lies the fact that the emotion is felt collectively, the rite is performed by a band or chorus who dance together *with a common leader*. Round that leader the emotion centres. When there is an act of Carrying-out or Bringing-in he either is himself the puppet or he carries it. Emotion is of the whole band; drama doing tends to focus on the leader. This leader,

[18]Harrison, 49.
[19]*AH*, 88.
[20]*AH*, 95–96.

this focus is then remembered, thought of, imaged; from being *per*ceived year by year he is finally *con*ceived. . . .

Had there been no periodic festivals, personification might long have halted. But it is easy to see that a recurrent *per*ception helps to form a permanent abstract *con*ception. The different actual recurrent May Kings and "Deaths," *because they recur,* get a sort of permanent life of their own and become beings apart.[21]

The May King in the Greek ritual dance is akin to the interlocutor or solo jig dancer in the minstrel show: both express collective emotion and so owe their force to the group they represent; both turn into abstract types rather than individual personalities; both persist despite the passage of time; both ultimately belong to the realm of myth or legend. From the attributes Rourke ascribed to the interlocutor one can readily deduce the antithetical terms in which Brooks criticized American society—its lack of social unity, its inability to move beyond the concrete demands of the business world, and, again, its absence of tradition and "spiritual experience." Rourke's reading of Harrison afforded her a striking refutation of all those charges.

Harrison's theory also provided Rourke a way of defending America even if Brooks were correct. The view of myth as originating in primitive ritual allowed Rourke to make an additional, important claim: that America was a nascent culture. Her statement in *American Humor* that "Far from having no childhood, the American nation was having a prolonged childhood"[22] spoke directly to Brooks' declaration that "we were founded by full-grown, modern, self-conscious men,"[23] and sharply illustrates the polemical aspect of Rourke's writings. But that same statement, taken together with her remarks in an unpublished essay that "we are a young people, with a riotous imagination" and that "all peoples in their youth invent mythologies,"[24] betrays Rourke's own concern with ultimately meeting European standards of culture and represents a concession to Brooks. For though our myths signified the "secure beginnings of a native poetry and a native language,"[25] insuring that we might eventually rival the Greeks, by implication we still lagged far behind the Europeans in literature and the fine arts. Nevertheless such a concession entailed its own line of defense: it was too early to demand completions. Our youth excused our inferior efforts.

Yet Rourke did not limit her understanding of the term "myth" to Harrison's sense of "primitive, necessary, universal foundation for culture." The work of another figure, Ruth Benedict, permitted Rourke to exonerate na-

---

[21]Harrison, 72.
[22]*AH*, 138.
[23]Brooks, "The Wine of the Puritans," 3, 8.
[24]"Old American Theatricals," CR Papers.
[25]Rourke, "American Art: A Possible Future," in *The Roots of American Culture*, 276.

tive culture by leading her to precisely the opposite conclusion: that America was unique. Rourke and Benedict may have known each other as Vassar undergraduates in the years 1905 to 1907. They did meet, however casually, no later than 1931. At that time, Benedict was about to embark on her *Patterns of Culture* (1934), a book which widely popularized the view among anthropologists known as "historical particularism."[26] As a disciple of Franz Boas, Benedict represented a divergence from nineteenth-century treatments of cultures as uniformly evolving through discrete steps from the primitive to the more advanced. Benedict's relativistic perspective and her insistence that one needed to examine a culture as a totality formed the basis of her appeal for Rourke. For if, as Benedict claimed, every culture exhibited a different "pattern," critics were wrong to base their convictions about America's inferiority on the fact that we had failed to produce classic painting or the English novel. In her "History of American Culture," Rourke planned to argue at length that we had made the unwarranted equation of "culture" with "literary culture," and had defined the arts in terms of "luxuries." We had erroneously assumed that our pattern would be the same as Europe's. Instead, Benedict's framework sanctioned, indeed demanded, the treatment of what Rourke called the "practical arts"—frontier architecture, folk design, work songs—as achievements of our culture.

Benedict's theory licensed Rourke to make an even bolder move. Margaret Mead has reported that Benedict "saw primitive cultures as in themselves works of art to be preserved for the world."[27] Rourke adopted a similar stance toward the American's creation of mythical characters. Early in *American Humor,* she quoted Henri Bergson's formulation of the origins of the comic as appearing "just when society and the individual, freed from the worry of self-preservation, begin to regard themselves as works of art." "With his triumphs fresh and his mind noticeably free," Rourke added, "by 1815 the American seemed to regard himself as a work of art, and began that embellished self-portraiture which nations as well as individuals may undertake."[28] Rourke's characterization, following Bergson, of the mythic Yankee, backwoodsman, and minstrel as artistic achievements was as effective a refutation of Brooks as the idea that we were a nascent culture: in a few brief years of national life—without a long prelude of primitive, pre-artistic expression—we had managed to create a special form of art.

Rourke's simultaneous reliance on Harrison and Benedict points to several traits of her work as a whole. First, by arriving at the contradictory conclusions that America was both primitive and specially advanced,

---

[26]See Marvin Harris, *The Rise of Anthropological Theory: A History of Theories of Culture* (New York: Thomas Y. Crowell Company, 1968).

[27]Margaret Mead, *Ruth Benedict* (New York: Columbia Univ. Press, 1974), 48.

[28]*AH,* 12–13.

Rourke exhibited all the characteristic coloration of the provincial, at once imitative and heedless of comparisons, cowering and boastful.[29] (Examination of her general definition of culture reveals the same tension at work.) Second, Rourke's amalgamation of the sources she read illustrates her practice of making theoretical writings serve her own intellectual ends, at the expense of precise definition. Though she was undoubtedly aware of contemporary debates among anthropologists and "myth critics" about the exact nature of myth, she used the term naively. But Rourke's naiveté served her well. Her inexact, eclectic approach is a clue that she seized upon the idea of myth out of more than a desire to construct a reasoned defense of American culture. Additionally, she saw in myth-making the promise of certain emotional comforts, both for artists and for critics like herself.

For though Rourke knew that myth originated in social coherence, it also promised to foster stronger social bonds, endowing random, disconnected events with unity and order, even drawing together a divided society. Rourke had recognized the integrative aspects of myth in *American Humor*. Noting the way in which Mark Twain drew upon the fantasies of the Yankee, Californian, and backwoodsman, giving his work "nation-wide scope," she added: "The wide reach may be unimportant for judgments of intrinsic quality, but its significance may be great among people seeking the illusive goal of unity and the resting-place of a tradition."[30] Elsewhere she observed:

Laughter created ease, and even more, a sense of unity, among a people who were not yet a nation and who were seldom joined in stable communities. These mythical figures partook of the primitive; and for a people whose life was still unformed, a searching out of primitive concepts was an inevitable and stirring pursuit, uncovering common purposes and directions.[31]

In fact, in his critique of *American Humor,* Bernard DeVoto found Rourke somewhat too interested in extracting social coherence from myth, "in danger of finding too much unity" in her characterization of native humor as fantasy and guilty of "pushing [her] original folk motif so far that it may discount individual originality and saltation."[32] Though Rourke rightly denied the specific charge, claiming that she had differentiated among varieties of humor, DeVoto had indeed sensed an impulse in her which a broad concept of myth could satisfy.

Myth's unifying function was especially important to the artist in danger

[29]See John Clive and Bernard Bailyn, "England's Cultural Provinces: Scotland and America," *William and Mary Quarterly,* 3rd Ser., 11, No. 2 (April 1954), 200-13.

[30]*AH,* 219-20.

[31]*AH,* 99.

[32]DeVoto to Rourke, [1931], CR Papers. In her reply Rourke accused DeVoto of being himself "a victim to the urge for simplification" in making Southwestern humor characterize American humor generally. Rourke to DeVoto, March 3, 1932, CR Papers.

of alienation from society. A sense of participation in socially-created myths could break the spell of isolation from the dominant culture, substituting a share in the collective imagination for the lonely confines of personality. Rourke incorporated into her reassuring concept of the connections among myth, artist, and society T. S. Eliot's idea of the function of tradition. For Rourke the terms "myth" and "tradition" shaded into one another, since she saw the creation and perpetuation of myths as the American's principal traditional activity. At the end of *American Humor,* she quoted directly from Eliot's "Tradition and the Individual Talent":

> The writer must know, as Eliot has said, "the mind of his own country—a mind which he learns in time to be much more important than his own private mind." . . . The difficult task of discovering and diffusing the materials of the American tradition—many of them still buried—belongs for the most part to criticism; the artist will steep himself in the gathered light. In the end he may use native sources as a point of radical departure; he may seldom be intent upon early materials; but he will discover a relationship with the many streams of native character and feeling. The single writer—the single production—will no longer stand solitary or aggressive but within a natural sequence.[33]

Though Rourke knew, with Eliot, that the future of art depended on the artist's thorough grounding in tradition, in this passage she emphasized the "relationship" tradition constructed between the potentially isolated artist and "his own country" by demanding, in Eliot's phrase, the "continual extinction of personality."[34] No image better captures the hope the discovery of a tradition of myth-making offered Rourke than her phrase "the artist will steep himself in the gathered light"; it promised warmth, abundance, clarity, immersion, illumination of place, and direction.

But myth might accomplish even more: it might provide the critic with the vital role of explicator. For if the critic accorded myth the power to insure art and social coherence, he could also charge himself with the important responsibility of interpreting and disseminating those myths to a culture dependent on them for sustenance. Rourke was aware that her view of myth and tradition rescued the critic from the position of ineffectual, expendable commentator on someone else's work and awarded him an indispensable social function. She elaborated on her statement that the task of discovering a native tradition "belongs for the most part in criticism"[35] in an unpublished essay entitled "The Decline of the Novel," which incidentally makes clear her interchangeable use of "tradition" and words related to myth:

> The function of criticism has been exalted by critics from Matthew Arnold on; the

[33]*AH, 302.*
[34]T. S. Eliot, "Tradition and the Individual Talent" (1919), in *Selected Essays,* new ed. (New York: Harcourt, Brace and World, 1960), 7.
[35]*AH,* 302.

major claim has been advanced that criticism can and does prepare the way for literature. But the proof of this has been lacking. . . . Yet there would seem to be a function which criticism could now fulfill. . . . The possibilities of the new subject matter [an exploration of "primary forms" like myth] . . . are endless. Perhaps in spite of its pretensions, criticism cannot or will not illuminate those interpretations. But one thing, surely, it can accomplish, and that is fully to open the perspectives within which these contemporary achievements [in literature] lie: A new and abundant tradition exists in our literature if this can only be extricated from the mass of preconceptions, inferior work, and a widespread belief that our past accomplishment is minor. Tradition, even in new literatures, has always formed a basic soil; ours is rich enough if it can only be fully seen. Out of a living perspective those epics, sagas, allegories, tales in which the imagination offers something for men to live by might come into that startling force and imagination which would seem their natural destiny in time of revolution. By interpreting its living alliances, criticism might even create a faith in our literature.[36]

Here the phrase "in time of revolution" indicates the political dimension of the critic's role. But the broader social and aesthetic importance of the critic is also clear: he is the person responsible for assembling myths in proper perspective so that they foster social cohesion and nurture art.

Like her willingness to consider America as primitive and her ready embrace of anything corroborating a native myth-making tendency, Rourke's attraction to what might be called the psychological benefits of myth—for the artist, the critic, and for society as a whole—tinges her defense of American culture with a tentative quality, as if Brooks were right after all. In the most explicit (albeit fragmentary) reference Rourke made to Brooks' sense of disunities within American life, she wrote in her notes, "Two levels, highbrow, lowbrow, to bring them together," followed by the phrase "what a set of writers could do."[37] That juxtaposition indicates that unity was a goal rather than an accomplished fact.

Since her remark falls in a section of "A History of American Culture" calling for nonacademic explorations of native traditions, the "set of writers" Rourke had in mind would seem to have consisted of critics like herself. She judged the existence of a "sensitive historical criticism" nothing less than a "major necessity"[38] if American culture were to flourish. That the explication of our myths promised not "comfort" or "solace" but long and difficult effort—"a concerted archaeology"[39] requiring selfless dedication—glorified the role of the critic all the more. It is interesting, along these lines, to look at the passage which was to have preceded Rourke's ac-

---

[36] "The Decline of the Novel," CR Papers.
[37] "A History of American Culture," CR Papers.
[38] Rourke, "American Art: A Possible Future," 295.
[39] Rourke, *Charles Sheeler: Artist in the American Tradition* (New York: Harcourt, Brace, 1938), 58.

knowledgments in "American Culture": "Those of us who have embarked
upon these controversial subjects in this generation almost constitute a
guild; we often do not know each other except by our writings, yet we make a
coterie."[40] Rourke's assertion that she belonged to a tightly-knit group may
have derived in part from a desire to combat her own loneliness. However
deliberate and self-willed her removal from academic circles, she did spend
most of her life in Grand Rapids, Michigan, apart from other writers and
scholars. But the terms "guild" and "coterie" endow her critical efforts with
a stature and dignity which the average American, if he knew of her
activities at all, would probably not confer upon them. Her words reflect the
hope, if not the fact, that she occupied a distinct and exclusive place and
function in American life.

Propelled by the many attractions of myth, Rourke set about to safeguard
the permanence of an American mythology. On that account, she drew upon
legends surrounding figures like Davy Crockett, Lotta Crabtree, and Audubon to proclaim the American myth-making tendency. But as if on the
chance that the fables she discovered might be too sparse to constitute a rich
mythology, Rourke also worked, both stylistically and through choice of
subject, to create American myths and traditions herself. Consider, for
example, the opening paragraph of *American Humor:*

> Toward evening of a midsummer day at the latter end of the eighteenth century a
> traveler was seen descending a steep red road into a fertile Carolina valley. He
> carried a staff and walked with wide, fast, sprawling gait, his tall shadow cutting
> across the lengthening shadows of the trees. His head was crouched, his back long;
> a heavy pack lay across his shoulders.[41]

In this passage, Rourke is engaged in spinning a yarn about the Yankee peddler in order to confirm and perpetuate his mythical attributes. While the
content of Rourke's argument declares that the Yankee was a mythical
creature, the form in which she casts that argument guarantees that it is so.
Her style adds to the myth, creating it anew. Perhaps by recording myths in
the style of the myth-maker Rourke could somehow crystallize them once
and for all, insuring their place as part of a permanent tradition.

The same use of style as a way of revitalizing myth appears in Rourke's
treatment of Crabtree, Audubon, and Crockett as fictional characters, and
partly explains her heavy reliance on the words "seems" and "as if"
throughout *American Humor,* which lend an aspect of unreality to her writing. Rourke also sought to establish American traditions (rather than simply
to report them) by characterizing as "traditional" virtually every intellectual movement about which she wrote: Marxist literary criticism, sym-

[40]"A History of American Culture," CR Papers.
[41]*AH,* 3.

bolism and surrealism, interest in biography, even attitudes toward World War I. The willful, boundless fabrication of traditions, which colors her literary judgments as well, is a variation on Rourke's adoption of the role of myth-maker in order to strengthen the basis for art and social unity.

Though Rourke typified the critic as myth-maker, she recognized that she was not alone in that enterprise. Many writers in the 1930s, suffering from a keen sense of social disintegration, turned to myth as a way of restoring order to what seemed an irrational world. Warren Susman has characterized the period of the Depression as a Jungian age, an era dominated by "a search for metaphysical certainty, a search for a sense of transcendent being, a collective identity deeply responding to deeply felt needs and aspirations. . . . It was an age which consciously sought new heroes, new symbols, even new myths" as a means of coping with what many perceived as the exposure of the American way of life.[42] According to Richard H. Pells, their need to understand the meaning of the Depression propelled Carl Sandburg, Archibald MacLeish, authors of WPA guidebooks, and even Brooks, among others, toward the exploration of the American past; in Pell's words, they transformed the past into "precisely the sort of compelling 'political myth' that could comfort the populace in an age of chaos and uncertainty."[43]

But to place Rourke (as Pells has done) in the company of those who, because of the psychological consequences of the Depression, looked for native myths is to misrepresent Rourke's early, and most significant, writing. The theme of myth appeared in Rourke's published work as far back as 1920 (the year she wrote an article about Paul Bunyan for the *New Republic*); by the time she began *American Humor* (presumably the late 1920s, since the book appeared in March, 1931), the depiction of Americans as myth-makers had already become her central preoccupation. While the Depression may have heightened her awareness of the unifying function of myth, adding to her sense that she was performing a vital task, in Rourke's case economic crisis bore no causal relation to intellectual concern.

Rather, years before Americans had grasped the seriousness of the Depression, writings as diverse as those of Brooks, Herder, Harrison, and Eliot had converged to provide her with an awareness of the aesthetic and cultural uses of a tradition of myth-making. If that haphazard convergence is a mark of Rourke's naiveté, vitiating her usefulness as an original contributor to our theories of myth or even as literary critic, it nevertheless enhances her significance for the historian. The contradictions, the defensive moves permeating Rourke's writings are signs of a struggle to define the in-

---

[42] Warren Susman, ed., *Culture and Commitment, 1929-1945* (New York: George Braziller, 1973), 19.

[43] Richard H. Pells, *Radical Visions and American Dreams* (New York: Harper and Row, 1973), 315.

tellectual's place in American society, and her complex striving tells us more than the simple phrase "the search for a usable past" conveys. Other aspects of Rourke's work—for example, her general view of cultural development, her aesthetic standards, her relationship to what she saw as "genteel" criticism, her writing style itself—lend themselves to similar consideration with an eye to the context from which her ideas sprang. Such an approach clarifies further the anxieties, and achievements, of those who, especially in the 1920s and 1930s, urged attention to native traditions in order to make (in Rourke's phrase) "a world out of a wilderness"[44]—a world in which culture would flourish, the artist would prosper, and the critic would reign.*

[44]Rourke, *Trumpets of Jubilee* (New York: Harcourt, Brace, 1927), 432. The phrase suggests a central metaphor in Lewis Mumford's *The Golden Day* (New York: Boni and Liveright, 1926), which heavily influenced Rourke.

*I am grateful to David Brion Davis, Donald Meyer, and Warren Susman for their help with earlier versions of this essay. Material from the Constance Rourke Papers and from the letters of Bernard DeVoto appears by the kind permission of Mrs. Carl Shoaff and Mrs. Bernard De-Voto, respectively.

"HISTORY WITH LIGHTNING": THE FORGOTTEN FILM *WILSON*

THOMAS J. KNOCK
Princeton University

WOODROW WILSON LOVED THE MOVIES. ONE OF THE FIRST HE EVER SAW was D. W. Griffith's momentous Civil War epic *Birth Of A Nation* (1915), which supposedly drew from the President the remark, "It is like writing history with lightning." Thereafter, Wilson went to the motion picture theater occasionally, sharing a pastime which became increasingly popular with Americans during his administration. In the last months of his presidency, while recovering from a paralytic stroke, he saw movies in the East Room as part of the diversionary therapy which his doctors prescribed.[1] As he sat convalescing, broken by the strain of the "Great War for Democracy" and his failure to convince the Senate and the American people that the United States should join the League of Nations, Wilson could hardly have guessed that the story of his life and his crusade for world peace would be resurrected upon the screen during a second world war which he had prophesied.

Many motion pictures about the country's favorite historical figures, including several presidents, have been produced over the years. But of the many sweeping pageants emanating from Hollywood, none approached the multilevel political and historical significance of the screen story about the twenty-eighth president. Heralded by its promoters as "The Most Important Event in Fifty Years of Motion Picture Entertainment," this 1944 production of Darryl F. Zanuck and Twentieth Century-Fox, a fervent mission on behalf of international cooperation, was the most talked-about picture of the year, receiving more critical praise and journalistic coverage than any other up to that time, with the possible exception of *Birth Of A Nation* and *Gone With The Wind* (1939). *Wilson* has been neglected in histories of the motion picture and in writings on American popular culture, but it was

[1]Lewis Jacobs, *The Rise of the American Film: A Critical History* (New York: Teachers College, 1939), 175; Gene Smith, *When The Cheering Stopped* (New York: Morrow, 1964), 137–39.

enormously significant—mainly because, along with *Birth Of A Nation, Intolerance* (1916), *All Quiet On The Western Front* (1930), and *Citizen Kane* (1941), it was among the first few American films which attempted to raise public political consciousness. Released just as World War II was coming to an end, during a period when over half the American population went to the movies each week, *Wilson* was pregnant with meaning for its audiences because of its theme of peace and its implied plea for the future United Nations; one New York review headlined *Wilson* as "The Movie To Prevent World War Three."[2]

Yet as the overwhelming majority of observers claimed that the film represented "Hollywood at the crossroads . . . of mature responsibilities"[3] there nevertheless were partisan voices calling for its censorship. The charge that *Wilson* was "Fourth Term Propaganda" for Franklin Delano Roosevelt created consternation for the United States Army and the Senate; and it elicited an act of Congress before the matter was settled. *Wilson* is of historical interest for other reasons. In addition to being one of Hollywood's best screen biographies, the film is also notable because it parallels the Wilson historiography of the day, which concentrated favorably on Wilson's career at Princeton University, and as president during the war, the Paris peace negotiations, and his fight for the League of Nations. On a vast popular scale the film enhanced the image of Wilson and his administration, which had fallen into disrepute in the 1930s. It also stimulated the rebirth of interest in both the President himself and in books published about him in the mid-forties.

Then too, few "behind the scenes" stories of the making of a historical motion picture are as fascinating as *Wilson's*. Mounting a huge production that required restaging the 1912 Democratic National Convention, building facsimiles of White House and Capitol Hill interiors, and designing thousands of period costumes, all photographed in Technicolor, constituted a tremendous technical challenge. No less difficult were those challenges of research and preparation for the screenplay, and selecting a cast to play highly sensitive, demanding roles.

* * *

That a major feature film about the life and times of Woodrow Wilson should be produced at all was essentially the idea of Darryl F. Zanuck. Zanuck had always been interested in making entertaining and educational movies about the lives of great people in history and had successfully

[2] *New York Times,* July 30, 1944, VI, 38 (full-page advertisement); *1945 Britannica Book of the Year* (Chicago, 1945), 460; *PM*, Aug. 3, 1944, 2.
[3] *Time,* Aug. 7, 1944, 84.

produced several before *Wilson*, including *Disraeli* (1929), *The House of Rothschild* (1934), *The Story of Alexander Graham Bell* and *Young Mister Lincoln* (1939). But he was most devoted to recent biography and politics. His political attitudes were contradictory: Zanuck had voted for Alf Landon in 1936, then became a close friend and frequent dinner guest of Franklin Roosevelt; yet in 1940 he campaigned for Wendell L. Willkie, his best friend in politics, who became chairman of the board of Twentieth Century-Fox in 1942.[4]

The producer conceived the idea for *Wilson* while working on an outline for a film about Samuel Gompers. Such a film, he believed, might help ameliorate current tensions between labor and management. While examining the part that Wilson played in Gompers' career it occurred to him that in the President there existed a subject of cinematic potential. The draft of a Wilson script was begun but Zanuck shelved it and the Gompers project when the United States entered the war.[5]

As a colonel in the Army Signal Corps, Zanuck served in the Aleutians and North Africa in 1942 and 1943. Like many others (including Roosevelt and Willkie) Zanuck believed that World War II was an outgrowth of the thwarting of Wilson's attempt to establish the League of Nations; that as the war was nearing an end, it seemed that history was repeating itself; that Wilson had, indeed, been a prophet. After the Office of War Information turned down his offer to make a documentary about Wilson and the League (because it was too ambitious and contained too many political traps), Zanuck returned undaunted to Hollywood in 1943 to film "The Woodrow Wilson Story." By explaining in stimulating pictorial terms America's failure to follow Wilson's lead, Zanuck hoped to vindicate the late President's counsel and thus help clear the path toward lasting peace for the new generation. He wanted to produce a full-length feature that provided entertainment along with an urgent message; in Hollywood terms: " . . . the story of a family [that became] the drama of the world!"[6]

To delineate the complex personality and career of Woodrow Wilson and interweave an issue of international concern into a palatable screen story was a task of Wilsonian proportions. Lamar Trotti, a seasoned writer with a flair for biography, took on the assignment. Trotti spent more than two years reading all the biographies and memoirs about Wilson in order to draft his screenplay. He also interviewed Josephus Daniels, Wilson's Secretary of

[4]Zanuck's best-known films include *The Grapes of Wrath* (1940), *Gentleman's Agreement* (1947), *All About Eve* (1950), and *The Longest Day* (1962). Mel Gussow, *Don't Say Yes Until I Finish Talking: A Biography of Darryl F. Zanuck* (New York: Doubleday, 1971), xv and 115–16.
[5]John Gassner and Dudley Nichols, eds., *Best Film Plays, 1943–44* (New York: Crown, 1944), "Preface to *Wilson*," by Darryl F. Zanuck, 1–2.
[6]Ibid.; Gussow, *Don't Say Yes*, 118; *New York Times,* July 30, 1944, VI, 38.

Navy, Miles McCahill of the Secret Service, and others who provided
different perspectives. Eleanor Wilson McAdoo, the President's daughter,
served as an informal counselor on family activities and other matters.
Trotti also studied the collections of the Woodrow Wilson Foundation and
the Library of Congress, where he consulted with Katherine E. Brand, Special Custodian of the Wilson Papers.[7] But the screen writer's chief source
was Ray Stannard Baker and his eight-volume biography *Woodrow Wilson,
Life and Letters* (1927–1939) which had won the Pulitzer Prize in 1940, and
which, despite many weaknesses in critical analysis, is still used by students
and scholars. The leading authority on Wilson during the thirties and forties,
Baker was skeptical at first, but he read the lengthy preliminary script and
was pleased. Although he made many corrections and notations, he was impressed by the quality of the writing and with the serious "homework" Trotti
had done. Several revisions followed, each reviewed by Baker who became
an inspired adviser, captivated by the idea of conveying "to perhaps ninety
million people Woodrow Wilson's essential message." In October of 1943
the 74-year-old journalist-historian travelled from his Amherst, Massachusetts, home to Hollywood, where he worked as a consultant for five
months.[8]

Mrs. Wilson, whose own courtship would be reenacted on the screen, also
studied each version of the script. Like Baker's, all of Mrs. Wilson's suggestions were incorporated into the text. Before actual filming began, she wrote
to Baker that "the motion picture stands approved," words welcomed by all
concerned. Later she wrote to Zanuck, "Needless to add, my hopes for the
success of the picture are deeper than your own."[9]

With the script near completion, Zanuck sought a director and cast. One
of Fox's leading directors, Henry King, a favorite of Zanuck's, at first tried
to discourage the project. Many of Zanuck's associates believed that any
story about Wilson, which necessarily included the saga of the League of
Nations, must unavoidably take a position on a current political issue—isolationism versus internationalism. This, coupled with the problem of presenting the Democrats as "the good guys" and the Republicans as "the bad
guys," rendered the Wilson story far too controversial, especially during an
election year; in any circumstances it seemed, at best, a great financial risk.

[7]Lamar Trotti to Ray Stannard Baker, Feb. 2 and July 15, 1943, Ray Stannard Baker
Papers, Library of Congress; Dean Francis B. Sayre, Jr., Washington National Cathedral
(Wilson's first grandchild), to author, telephone interview, Feb. 25, 1974; Miss Katherine E.
Brand to author, telephone interview, Dec. 8, 1975; *Washington Post,* Sept. 6, 1944, B-8.
[8]Baker to Trotti, Mar. 10, May 17, June 6, and July 19, 1943; Trotti to Baker, Feb. 23, June
11, and July 25, 1943; Baker to Jason S. Joy, Sept. 16, 1943, Baker Papers; see also Robert C.
Bannister, Jr., *Ray Stannard Baker, The Mind and Thought of a Progressive* (New Haven: Yale
Univ. Press, 1966), 303.
[9]Mrs. Wilson to Baker, Nov. 8, 1943 and Feb. 5, 1944, Baker Papers; Mrs. Wilson to
Zanuck, Nov. 19, 1943, Edith Bolling Wilson Papers, Library of Congress, hereinafter cited as
Wilson Papers.

Plate 1: Reception at the White House. Left to Right: Robert Lansing (Stanley Logan); Wilson (Alexander Knox); Edith Wilson (Geraldine Fitzgerald); William Gibbs McAdoo (Vincent Price); Colonel House (Charles Halton); Prof. Henry Holmes (Charles Coburn).

Zanuck was not dissuaded and insisted that King read the script. King offered criticism, but liked it, and began directorial research by travelling to Princeton and Washington, D. C.[10]

Gathering the right cast for *Wilson* was difficult (see Plate 1). The role of Woodrow Wilson was monumental. The character would appear in 294 scenes and deliver 1,124 lines, including 338 speeches (verbatim excerpts from Wilson's own addresses). Casting the most suitable actor in the longest male role in screen history was crucial; Zanuck agreed with Mrs. Wilson that "it must be someone worthy of it!" The producer considered William Powell and Ronald Colman but soon decided not to seek a "star" name; he wanted an actor who would make a believable Wilson.[11] Alexander Knox, a 37-year-old Canadian actor had heard about the project and made a taping of the dialogue. His interpretation "proved so moving and dramatic . . . "

[10]Zanuck to Mrs. Wilson, Nov. 15, 1943, Wilson Papers; S. A. Israel to Baker, Feb. 11, 1945, Baker Papers; Gassner and Nichols, *Best Film Plays,* "Preface to *Wilson,*" 2–3; *New York Times,* July 2, 1944, II, 3.

[11]Mrs. Wilson to Baker, Nov. 8, and Baker to Wilson, Nov. 13, 1943, Baker Papers; Zanuck to Wilson, Nov. 15, 1943, Wilson Papers; *Collier's,* July 22, 1944, 47.

that Zanuck gave him the part. Unknown at the time, Knox became famous almost overnight as Wilson. Curiously, like Wilson, he was of Scotch-Irish ancestry, the son of a Presbyterian minister, and as a youth, like Wilson, had privately studied elocution. To prepare for the part, Knox became an ardent student of Wilson, attempting to bring both intellectual and artistic understanding to his portrayal.[12]

To play Edith Bolling Wilson, the strong-minded widow whom Wilson married sixteen months after the death of his beloved first wife, Ellen Axson (Ruth Nelson) in August 1914, Zanuck chose Geraldine Fitzgerald. "She's an independent young lady," said Mrs. Wilson approving of the choice, "and she will do for the part." In order to bring a dimension of humanness to their relationship, Fitzgerald, after reading Mrs. Wilson's autobiography, decided to treat the character of "Woodrow" not as the President, but as her husband, her lover, who happened also to be a great man.[13]

Sir Cedric Hardwicke played Henry Cabot Lodge of Massachusetts, Wilson's famous archenemy who chaired the Senate Foreign Relations Committee. Trotti constructed the character primarily from the Brahmin's own work, *The Senate and the League of Nations*, from the transcripts of the signal three-hour meeting of August 19, 1919, between Wilson and Lodge and the Committee during the League controversy, and from Mrs. Wilson's autobiography. In *Wilson* Lodge bears the blame for the failure of the United States to enter the League. Despite the villain-like profile, Lodge's namesake grandson felt that the characterization reflected his grandfather's viewpoint honestly, and consented to the portrayal.[14]

With permission secured from the heirs of 96 historical figures, and with a total of 148 speaking parts cast, including Thomas Mitchell as Joseph P. Tumulty and Vincent Price as William Gibbs McAdoo, production of *Wilson* commenced. As Zanuck made preparations, he worried that the picture might be dubbed "for 'highbrows' only." He thought that in order to be successful at the box office entertainment values would have to be underscored. Hence, his and director King's conception became a lavishly designed, Technicolored spectacle. The riotous Baltimore convention of 1912 (where Wilson was nominated for President on the forty-sixth ballot), for example, took place full-scale for entertainment's sake at the Los Angeles Shrine Au-

[12]Gassner and Nichols, *Best Film Plays,* "Preface to *Wilson,*" 5; James Hilton, "Alexander Knox, A Rather Remarkable Man," *Photoplay* (February 1945), 42–43 and 94–95; see also "Introductory Remarks—Wilson Film" (speech by Baker at Winter Park, Florida, Feb. 27, 1945), Baker Papers.

[13]Edith Bolling Wilson, *My Memoir* (Indianapolis: Bobbs-Merrill, 1939); *New York Times,* July 30, 1944, II, 3.

[14]Henry Cabot Lodge, *The Senate and the League of Nations* (New York: Scribner's Sons, 1925); Trotti to Zanuck, Nov. 9, 1943, copy of memorandum in Baker Papers; *Newsweek,* Aug. 14, 1944, 72; *Collier's,* July 22, 1944, 47.

ditorium. Alive with cheers and marching bands, the scene required six filming days, 34 trucks filled with electrical equipment, and banners, placards,
and 1912-style seersuckers, and over 1,500 conventioneers (see Plate 2). To
backdrop other events in Wilson's life 126 sets were built, including reproductions of the House of Representatives Chamber, the East, Blue, and
Oval Rooms, the Hall of Mirrors at Versailles, and hundreds of replicas of
White House set pieces. After the scores of players said their lines and an
additional 16,000 extras passed before the cameras during 90 days of shooting, Zanuck and his film editor worked for weeks to put the pieces together.
The extravaganza cost more to make than Fox had ever grossed on any previous production; at the then unheard-of price tag of $5,200,000, it became
the most expensive motion picture in history.[15]

Zanuck had devoted two years of his life to supervising all aspects of the
venture while overseeing other Fox efforts. His concern and expectations for
Wilson were boundless. "It was the *only* time I saw him on . . . [any] set,"
said Henry King. *Wilson* had become Zanuck's personal crusade for world
peace, in the belief that it would serve a great purpose for the country. Yet
with so much corporate money at stake, he had also to think about his stock-
holders. Consequently, Zanuck launched the publicity "campaign of the
century" to insure a healthy return on the record investment, and, ever the
man with a social conscience, the popular dissemination of the principles of
Woodrow Wilson. Illustrated features and full-page advertisements were
published in so many national magazines that their combined circulation
covered the entire American population. Across the nation 3,280 spot radio
announcements were broadcast during a four-week period. "*Wilson* Is Coming" in a 50' × 75' montage decorated the Fifth Avenue side of the Roxy
Theater; 32,000 smaller billboards advertised it from coast to coast. For the
gala August 1 premiere Zanuck summoned the cast members and other
movie people, presidents of major corporations, leading newspaper
publishers, prominent politicians, surviving members of the Wilson family
and Cabinet, and 200 members of the Woodrow Wilson Foundation. George
Jessel, master of ceremonies for the publicity broadcast carried by eight
New York radio stations, greeted Mrs. Wilson, Eleanor Wilson McAdoo,
Ray Stannard Baker, Bernard Baruch, and Josephus Daniels, as well as
Wendell Willkie, Sumner Welles, Henry Luce, Henry Morganthau, Jr., and
many others.[16] At that point Zanuck felt he had created a masterpiece, "the
most significant film . . . since *Birth Of A Nation*," but grimly quipped that

[15]Ibid., 18; Gassner and Nichols, *Best Film Plays*, 4–5; *New York Times*, Mar. 5, 1944, II, 3,
and Mar. 26, 1944, VI, 18–19; *Time*, Aug. 7, 1944, 84 (fn.). The budget included a million for
promotion; *Gone With The Wind* had cost $4,250,000 to produce.
[16]*Motion Picture Herald*, July 29, 1944, 35–37, and Aug. 5, 1944, 20; *Box Office Digest*, July
18, 1944, 10; *Motion Picture Daily*, July 24, 1944, 1 and 6; *Hollywood Reporter*, Aug. 2, 1944, 1
and 11.

Plate 2: The Democratic National Convention as recreated by cinematographer Leon Shamroy.

unless *Wilson* was "successful from every standpoint, I'll never make another film without Betty Grable." And so, with "the eyes of the world . . . on the premiere," the epic story of *Wilson* unreeled publicly for the first time.[17]

The picture opens upon Woodrow Wilson, President of Princeton University, when the New Jersey political boss calls on the professor to offer him the Democratic gubernatorial nomination. After Wilson ultimately crosses 1600 Pennsylvania Avenue, the death of his wife, the outbreak of war in Europe, Cabinet debates over the sinking of the Lusitania and American neutrality, and Wilson's marriage to Edith Bolling Galt are all sketched episodically.

His reelection triumph over Charles Evans Hughes, based on the slogan "He kept us out of war!" is followed by the German resumption of unrestricted submarine warfare as of February 1, 1917. Wilson's ringing war message (a condensed version taken from Wilson's April 2, 1917 address) portends the solemn purpose of the remainder of the film. "For Democracy . . . for a universal dominion of right by such a concert of free peoples as shall bring peace and safety to all nations and make the world itself at last free," Wilson asserts, are America's reasons for entering the conflict. After months of war to end all wars, the announcement of the Fourteen Points brings about the Armistice, whence Wilson's overwhelming European reception and the Battle of Versailles are encapsulated in "March of Time" newsreels, intercut with reenactments of the deliberations of the "Big Four." Wilson returns home with the League of Nations, which he believes can maintain peace in the world. But Senatorial opposition to the treaty, led by Henry Cabot Lodge, stands in the way. The President feels compelled to stump the country, to tell "the people" what is at stake, and rally them behind the cause. He declares that America's isolation has come to an end and warns the people of a more dreadful war to come if the League is discarded. Soon after the strenuous campaign he suffers a stroke, and with Harding's election, the League is lost. On Inauguration Day at the Capitol, Wilson, a semi-invalid, defeated but resolute, assures his Cabinet that the ideals of the League will never die, conceding to Providence that "it may come about in a *better* way than we proposed." With that, as Edith takes his arm, "Wilson walks out of the room—into history."[18]

Wilson received a standing ovation at the Roxy. The story does not seem as significant and unusual today as it did then. But nothing like *Wilson* had ever before been seen on the screen. Before and during the Second World

---

[17]Zanuck to Mrs. Wilson, July 13, 1944, Wilson Papers; Gussow, *Don't Say Yes,* 115; *Motion Picture Herald,* July 29, 1944, 40.

[18]Gassner and Nichols, *Best Film Plays* (*Wilson* by Lamar Trotti), 86; Caption attached to *Wilson* still, Motion Picture Section, Library of Congress.

Plate 3: Wilson addressing the Joint Session of Congress.

War the staple American film diet consisted mainly of light comedies, action–adventures backdropped by the war, musicals, love stories, and other kinds of escapist fare. *Wilson* was different. Presented on a spectacular scale, it was the first American film ever to assay the deeds of actual politicians still living or of recent memory. To its initial audiences *Wilson* was thought-provoking and timely. An unusual motion picture, ostensibly intended for the purpose of entertainment, it interpreted recent events in world history, and promoted a controversial solution to the tragic problem of global war.

The critical response to the film was unprecedented. Leading publications throughout the country observed its advent with a sense of excitement and urgency. *Life* magazine typified the tidal wave of praise with a cover story about *Wilson*, calling it "one of the best pictures Hollywood ever made." *Newsweek* magazine reported that "Darryl F. Zanuck scores one of Hollywood's rare triumphs. . . . " *Time* described the film as "extremely absorbing, significant, and entertaining" and declared that "Millions are likely to be excited and moved by it." The *Washington Star* described it as "intellectually stimulating," and "proof of what the movies can do when guided by intelligence," after *Wilson* opened in the nation's Capitol amid much pomp and hoopla. And the *Washington Post* regarded it as "one of the most distinguished films in the whole history of the cinema."[19]

Commentators stressed two major points—the image of Woodrow Wilson created by the film, and the political and moral question, one of grave consequence to the America of 1944, posed by the film. Recognizing the limits placed on a 2½-hour-long movie, Knox managed to define a credible, sympathetic hero, an intellectual, professorial man possessing warmth, wit, integrity, and courage. Humanizing the image of Wilson was vital to the film's success if audiences were to accept its thesis. Within Trotti's dramatic construction Knox builds favorable sentiment in intimate scenes emphasizing Wilson's devotion to his family, his enjoyment of football, golf, and vaudeville, his grief at his wife's death, and his happiness when he remarries. Convincing the audience not only of Wilson's goodness but his greatness as well, Knox's interpretation of Wilson as President makes the personality study most impressive. The reading of the war message, for instance, in a reenactment replete with a Joint Session of Congress, is dramatic and portentous, underscored by Knox's brilliant elocution (see Plate 3). And the restrained emotion he brings to the speech of "mortification and shame" at Pueblo, Colorado, conveys the sense of epic tragedy of the end of Wilson's

[19]*Life,* Aug. 7, 1944, 53–56; *Newsweek,* Aug. 14, 1944, 72; *Time,* Aug. 7, 1944, 84–88; *Washington Star,* Sept. 8, 1944, B-12; *Washington Post,* Sept. 8, 1944, 16; *New York Daily News,* Aug. 2, 1944, 35; *Los Angeles Times,* Aug. 11, 1944, 12; *San Francisco Examiner,* Aug. 30, 1944, 8; *Boston Globe,* Sept. 29, 1944, 19.

career. Bosley Crowther of the *New York Times* characterized the critical opinion: "Much of the film's exceptional quality is due to the performance of Alexander Knox.... It is good to hear speeches spoken—especially Wilson's—with a clear and resonant voice. The casting of Mr. Knox ... in this role was truly inspired."[20]

The portrayal drew comment from Wilson's friends and family. Former Navy Secretary Josephus Daniels exclaimed that, although Knox's Wilson was not perfect, his lines were "delivered so impressively that one ... felt he was living over again those tense days." Mrs. Wilson, very pleased, wrote to Zanuck, "Every detail is perfect. ..." The rest of the family in general did not think that Knox actually sounded like Wilson or resembled him strikingly (the make-up consisted of little more than nose putty, hair oil, and pince-nez eyeglasses) but liked his performance and the film "fairly well"[21] (see Plate 4).

Of far greater importance than the quality of Alexander Knox's rendering of Wilson, and overshadowing the production values of the motion picture, was its examination of internationalism and isolationism. Before *Wilson* was completed Lamar Trotti had written to Ray Stannard Baker that

> It is our earnest hope that the men and women who see this picture ... [will understand] that here was a great man who fought and died for a great ideal ... a world united for peace through a League of Nations and that they will be awakened to the issues at stake, to the dangers of indifference, isolation, and reaction, so that the tragedy of the present war which the Wilson dream might have prevented, may never again be permitted to occur.

The point was lost on no one in the press. Marshall Field's *PM Daily*, which serialized the screenplay, considered it "without question, the most important picture of its time" because "*Wilson* may help to break the tragic pattern, to learn from the past ... to save a new generation.... " Arthur Sweetser, president of the Woodrow Wilson Foundation, wrote in *Changing World* that *Wilson* was perhaps "the most important single contribution to the education of the American public regarding America's place in world-life that has ever been made.... " *Springfield Republican* columnist David Lawrence, who had authored *The True Story of Woodrow Wilson* in 1924, stated that *Wilson* represented "a milestone ... in the teaching of American history to the people of this country." *Saturday Review* paid special tribute to *Wilson* by breaking its twenty-year-long policy of *not* reviewing movies; the editors strongly recommended the film, "convinced that this picture is a document of the first importance."[22]

    [20]*New York Times,* Aug. 2, 1944, 18.
    [21]Josephus Daniels, *Raleigh News and Observer,* Aug. 6, 1944, 4; Wilson to Zanuck, Sept. 9, 1944, Wilson Papers; Sayre to author, Feb. 25, 1974.
    [22]"Mr. Trotti's Memorandum," undated copy, Baker Papers; *PM,* Aug. 2, 1944, 20, and Aug. 3, 1944, 2–9; *Changing World,* Sept. 1944; *Springfield Republican,* Sept. 13, 1944, 13; *Saturday Review,* Aug. 12, 1944, 23–24.

Plate 4: Wilson signs the Treaty of Versailles.

Nor did Wilson scholars ignore the film. Baker, of course, was delighted with it (like Mrs. Wilson) and agreed with the journalistic responses. Other historians, however, later noted several distressing oversights and inaccuracies. Thomas A. Bailey, for example, author of *Woodrow Wilson and the Lost Peace* and *Woodrow Wilson and the Great Betrayal*, pointed out aptly that Hollywood glossed over Wilson's personal shortcomings, and oversimplified and fictionalized some details of the Wilson-Lodge feud, Wilson's dismissal of Count von Bernstorff, the German ambassador, and the campaign for the League.[23] Arthur S. Link, the dean of the Wilson scholars, noted in the first volume of his definitive multivolume biography of Wilson that the film erroneously credited William Jennings Bryan with securing the presidential nomination for Wilson at Baltimore. Both historians felt that Knox was effective but regretted the film's distractingly recurrent expositions of the Wilson family singing around the piano and the blaring of popular songs and marching bands.[24] Because the production spent so much

[23] *Woodrow Wilson and the Lost Peace* (New York: Macmillan, 1944); *Woodrow Wilson and the Great Betrayal* (New York: Macmillan, 1945); Wilson to Zanuck, Sept. 9, 1944, Wilson Papers; Baker to Trotti, Aug. 29, 1944, Baker Papers; Thomas A. Bailey, *Woodrow Wilson and the Great Betrayal*, vi and 114; Bailey to author, Mar. 2, 1974.

[24] Arthur S. Link, *Wilson: The Road to the White House* (Princeton: Princeton Univ. Press, 1947), 463; Link to author, interview at Princeton University, Nov. 25, 1975. Professor Link told me that he looked upon the film favorably. Regarding it as one of the better Hollywood biographies, and as an effective propaganda piece for the United Nations, he nonetheless found its inaccuracies regrettable.

time on entertainment and spectacle, historical omissions were inevitable. Partly because all of the primary research sources were not then open to the public, and especially because the politics of Wilson's era merged with the politics of the 1940s, a penetrating examination would hardly have been likely.

Despite the film's historical oversimplification, its main thrust—Wilson's vain, yet courageous, crusade for the League of Nations—carried dramatic force. Most contemporary writers, albeit not scholars, were satisfied with the essentials of the film and agreed with Bosley Crowther that *Wilson* was evidence of "the widening scope of Hollywood," and was bound to shake "some cobwebs loose from the 'safety first' policies" of Hollywood.[25]

The film also drew *editorial* comment from major newspapers. The *New York Post* opined that "This fine movie can play a great and important part in that long fight [for world peace], into which we have twice poured so much hope and so much blood." The message editorialized by the *Post,* and the *Nation,* the *Christian Science Monitor*, the *Chicago Sun-Times*, the *Philadelphia Record*, the *Atlanta Constitution*, and others, was that all America should see *Wilson*. Reflecting such assessments in the press, columnist Lee Morris, overwhelmed by the film, proclaimed on the front page of the *Philadelphia Record* that *Wilson* was "the motion picture that may conceivably change the history of the world."[26]

As the film began its peace march throughout the movie palaces of America, notes of partisan criticism and suppression were sounded. A month before Wilson's general release the *Washington Times-Herald*, an anti-New Deal paper, attacked Zanuck's production for being part of an alleged Hollywood–White House scheme to reelect Franklin D. Roosevelt for a fourth term. The paper asserted that *Wilson* would be "counted on heavily by some of the more enthusiastic New Dealers to swing public sentiment behind FDR. . . ." Released at the beginning of the Roosevelt-Dewey contest, *Wilson,* which glorified FDR's first political mentor (Roosevelt had served as Wilson's Assistant Secretary of Navy) and promoted his fourth-term peace platform, acquired a new meaning. Following the *Times-Herald* broadside, the conservative *Washington Daily News* accused Zanuck in an editorial entitled "Franklin Delano Wilson" of subtly modeling his Wilson characterization after Roosevelt in order to swing the election, and suggested that the Democratic National Committee ought to subsidize Twentieth Century-Fox.[27]

A registered Republican, Zanuck dismissed the charge as ridiculous. The so-called underlying political purpose of the film, he countered, could just as

[25] *New York Times,* Aug. 6, 1944, II, 1.
[26] *New York Post,* Aug. 3, 1944, 21; *Philadelphia Record*, Sept. 9, 1944, 1.
[27] *Washington Times-Herald,* July 13, 1944, 14; *Washington Daily News,* Aug. 3, 1944, 20.

easily be interpreted as propaganda for many leading liberal Republicans like Zanuck's close friend Wendell L. Willkie. An adamant anti-isolationist, Willkie in 1943 had written *One World*, a best-selling tract which recounted his recent global travels and called for international organization. Furthermore, Governor Dewey, the 1944 Republican nominee, had promised in his campaign speeches to uphold the social legislation of the New Deal and pursue an internationalist policy. *Wilson* was therefore "damned nonpartisan" according to Zanuck.[28]

Many publications sympathetic to the film and Zanuck's reasoning (*Time* and *Newsweek*, for example) nevertheless made at least passing note of the pro-Roosevelt charge. *PM*, which gave *Wilson* extensive coverage, did the film damage when it cumbrously topped a rave review with "*Wilson* Wartime Wisdom May Help Win For FDR." Shortly, the headline appeared on the front page of the *New York Times* that the "Army Bans *Wilson* As Film For Troops." The Morale Services Division of the War Department announced that the film would be banned in all troop camps in the United States and abroad because it contained material which might be construed as violating the Soldiers' Voting Act, a law which prohibited the distribution on military bases of motion pictures, radio programs, and periodicals of partisan political content.[29]

It was not long before Secretary of War Henry L. Stimson collected a stack of telegrams protesting the ban. The League of Nations Association wired Stimson that the censoring of *Wilson* only "would be expected in the German and Japanese armies." The CIO War Relief Committee, the National Maritime Union, and individuals including Senator A. B. Chandler of Kentucky and Spyros Skouras, president of Twentieth Century-Fox, protested to Stimson that the ban was unfair, that it amounted to "tyrannical censorship to be expected only from the most reactionary . . . government." A number of newspapers editorialized against the ban, and New York City Mayor Fiorello LaGuardia told reporters that the army's opinion of the film "simply did not make sense." Senator Theodore F. Green, Rhode Island Democrat, called the whole affair "foolishness . . . by Republicans," while even Senator Taft of Ohio admitted that the army interpretation of the law was "silly."[30]

The original purpose of the Soldiers' Voting Act, according to Taft, was to prevent standing administrations from using their communications monopoly to disseminate politically biased information to the armed forces. As he

[28]*Collier's*, July 22, 1944, 47.
[29]*PM*, Aug. 2, 1944, 2; *New York Times*, Aug. 10, 1944, 1 and 15.
[30]League of Nations Association to Stimson, Aug. 11, 1944, Arthur Sweetser Papers, Library of Congress; *New York Times*, Aug. 10, 1944, 1 and 15, and Aug. 11, 1944, 7, and Aug. 12, 1944, 1; *Los Angeles Times*, Aug. 11, 1944, II, 4.

explained on the floor of the Senate, after reading into the record the *Washington Daily News* attack, the trouble with *Wilson* arose because under the existing legislation the Army ruled that publications and films and the like sold or distributed within troop camps somehow made them *government-sponsored* publications and films. The open-ended regulations had created similar minor problems in the past, but with the Morale Division's "unnecessarily restrictive interpretation" of *Wilson* the deficiencies in the law were laid bare. Responding quickly to the numerous complaints, Taft and Green co-sponsored successful amendments to the Soldiers' Voting Act. The changes provided for the unhampered circulation within the armed forces of all "entertainment material as generally presented to the public in the United States."[31]

While *Wilson* influenced legislative deliberations on Capitol Hill it also made history at the box office. During its record-breaking run at the Roxy Theater more than 20,000 crowded in line daily to see the film; after five weeks in circulation over one million people (in New York, Los Angeles, and San Francisco) had paid to see it. By February of 1945 an estimated ten million people had seen *Wilson* in hundreds of theaters at advanced prices.[32]

Although it is impossible to precisely determine the real effect that *Wilson* may have had on its audiences, it contributed to the climate of internationalism. The film commanded the greatest numbers as World War II drew to its climax, and as discussions at Dumbarton Oaks, succeeded by the United Nations San Francisco Conference, took place during a period when the name of Woodrow Wilson echoed irresistibly from the past. As the Woodrow Wilson Foundation pointed out, *Wilson* "carried unmistakable parallelism to the eyes of millions throughout the country who might not have been reached by the printed word." Several contemporary observations substantiate this assertion. Josephus Daniels, for example, wrote that he felt that the opening night audience in New York "left the theater with the feeling that this generation must repair the errors which made possible the present holocaust." Convinced that *Wilson* was "going to have a great effect throughout the country," Arthur Sweetser wrote to Ray Stannard Baker and to Undersecretary of State Sumner Welles of the audience in Washington, D. C.: "Certainly people seemed deeply moved, reflective, even saddened" by the film. After a private showing at the White House President Roosevelt wrote to Sweetser that *Wilson* "is excellent and will have a splendid effect." Years later Secretary of State Cordell Hull recorded in his memoirs that he reminded the American delegation of the contemporary lesson which the film dramatized during an impasse in negotiations at Dumbarton Oaks. Darryl F. Zanuck received more letters

[31]U.S., Congress, *Congressional Record,* Senate, 78th Cong., 2nd sess., Aug. 15, 1944, 90, pt. 5: 6936–39; House, 6983 (Senate Bill 2050).

[32]S. A. Israel to Baker, Feb. 11, 1945, Baker Papers; *New York Times,* Aug. 10, 1944, 15, and Sept. 10, 1944, II, 1.

about *Wilson* than Twentieth Century-Fox usually received in response to any other half dozen pictures. From all over the world he gathered hundreds of notes from soldiers, sailors, and civilians, and even avowed isolationists who admitted that the film had impressed them. Similarly, Mrs. Wilson wrote to Baker that the film "does seem to have done a real service and my mail reflects that every day."[33]

No organized survey was ever conducted to determine the degree of influence *Wilson* wielded over its audiences. However, the *New Republic* reported that some curious interviewers questioned patrons who had just seen the film and found "a definite increase in cooperative spirit among the movie-goers." During the ban controversy *PM* asked servicemen outside the Roxy what they thought of the film. "I believe in the United Nations. I think everyone should see this picture," answered a 20-year-old sergeant who typified the responses regardless of the individuals' political affiliations, "so we won't make the mistake again that we made in 1920. That's what I am fighting for." The *New York Times'* Bosley Crowther later conducted his own survey. Many people he spoke with came out of the theater in tears; some said it was the most inspiring film they had ever seen. Regardless of age or occupation, all of the people he interviewed left the movie endorsing the philosophy of the League. Crowther related his findings to a poll taken in 1943 to ascertain the effects of the pro-Russian film *Mission to Moscow*, a semi-documentary Warner Brothers release based on the memoirs of Ambassador Joseph E. Davies, which "raised pro-Soviet sentiment . . . among those who saw it." He suggested that the residual power of *Wilson*, and its message of "It must not happen again," would be greater and more widespread, that millions would leave the film in "an anti-isolationist frame of mind."[34]

Public opinion polls tell us that a tremendous shift of opinion in favor of U. S. participation in some kind of world organization took place among Americans throughout World War II. As one historian has pointed out, Americans realized gradually that they had been given perhaps their last "second chance." The new public profile was formed by the experience of a second war (and the events surrounding it), changing government policies regarding international cooperation, and a variety of media. A measurable example of the latter was Wendell L. Willkie's *One World*, considered "the most influential book published during the war," and which "both reflected

[33] *Woodrow Wilson Foundation Annual Report, 1944–45*, 3; *Raleigh News and Observer*, Aug. 6, 1944, 4; Sweetser to Baker, Sept. 8, 1944, Sweetser to Welles, Sept. 11, 1944, Roosevelt to Sweetser, Sept. 6, 1944, Zanuck to Sweetser, undated typescript, Sweetser Papers; *The Memoirs of Cordell Hull* (New York: Macmillan, 1948), vol. II, 1703; Israel to Baker, Feb. 11, 1945, and Wilson to Baker, Dec. 25, 1944, Baker Papers.
[34] *New Republic*, Sept. 11, 1944, 295; *PM*, Aug. 10, 1944, 3; *New York Times*, Sept. 10, 1944, II, 1; see also Melvin Small, "Buffoons and Brave Hearts: Hollywood Portrays the Russians, 1939–1944," *California Historical Quarterly* (Winter 1973), 326–337.

and helped to create" the turn away from traditional isolationism.[35] Yet, as *Wilson* was seen by so many people—several times the 1.5 million that bought *One World*—one can reasonably conclude that despite the fact that it has been neglected as such, the film was just as important as Willkie's book or any other single major factor during the final stages of American popular conversion to active internationalism. Thus, the motion picture became the most widely circulated and the single most influential propaganda piece on behalf of the United Nations of the entire decade.

There was another distinctive development attributable to *Wilson*. During the war, for obvious reasons, allusions to the President and consequent scholarly examinations of his administration burgeoned as his stature as a great world statesman grew. The major literary works included Thomas A. Bailey's volumes, mentioned previously, Herbert C. F. Bell's *Woodrow Wilson and the People*, *The Economic Thought of Woodrow Wilson* by William Diamond, Dexter Perkins' *America and Two Wars*, and Gerald W. Johnson's picture biography, *Woodrow Wilson: The Unforgettable Figure Who Has Returned to Haunt Us*. More than 600,000 pamphlets, additionally, were published by the Wilson Foundation pertaining to Wilson and the prospects for world organization, not to mention countless newspaper and magazine articles. Ray Stannard Baker told H. C. F. Bell in late 1943 that he believed that Zanuck's *Wilson* would be of "the greatest value in reviving interest" in the subject. Ruth Cranston, author of *The Story of Woodrow Wilson*, informed Baker that Charles Scribner's Sons, for one, realized the potential. "We expect to publish in August [1945] about the time the Wilson picture is released to second run movie houses," she wrote. Scribner's also saw opportunity for a reissue of Baker's biography, originally published by Doubleday. Baker wrote a new preface to Scribner's "Potomac Edition" of *Life and Letters*, published at the end of 1945, which cited the picture as the primary factor responsible for the new public interest in Wilson. Within one year Scribner's had sold nearly as many sets of the books as Doubleday had in ten years.[36]

[35] *Public Opinion Quarterly* (Fall 1943), 498; (Summer 1944), 301; (Fall 1944), 454. Of the American public 26% favored American participation in some kind of international peace-keeping organization in 1937. In 1941, 38% were in favor; 72% supported the idea by 1944. See also Robert A. Divine's perceptive study, *Second Chance: The Triumph of Internationalism in America During World War II* (New York: Atheneum, 1967), particularly 103–07 and 167–71. Samuel Eliot Morison, Henry Steele Commager, and William E. Leuchtenburg, *The Growth of the American Republic* (New York: Oxford Univ. Press, 1969, 6th ed.), vol. II, 603.

[36] Herbert C. F. Bell, *Woodrow Wilson and the People* (Garden City: Doubleday, Doran, 1945); William Diamond, *The Economic Thought of Woodrow Wilson* (Baltimore: Johns Hopkins Univ. Press, 1943); Dexter Perkins, *America and Two Wars* (Boston: Little, Brown, 1944); Gerald W. Johnson, *Woodrow Wilson: The Unforgettable Figure Who Has Returned to Haunt Us* (New York: Harper, 1944); Ruth Cranston, *The Story of Woodrow Wilson* (New York: Simon and Schuster, 1945); *Wilson Foundation Annual Report, 1944–45*, 7–10; Baker to Bell, Nov. 26, 1943; Cranston to Baker, May 30, 1945, Wilson to Baker, Jan. 1, 1945, and Baker

Earning about three million dollars (an outstanding gross in 1944–45) on its road show and second run engagements, *Wilson* succeeded magnificently as a Hollywood documentary-feature on three levels: it composed effective propaganda for the United Nations, promoted a heroic image of Woodrow Wilson, and provided for its audiences a general, if simplistic, education in early twentieth-century American history. However, as commercial entertainment, Zanuck judged his work a failure, based on the amount of money it cost to make compared to what it earned, and his criterion of complete success—acceptance by "the widest audience possible." When the film left the big cities on the east and west coasts to tour middle America and the hinterlands, it lost all of its momentum. At a time when most people went to the movies solely for relaxation, to see their favorite stars and escape into lands of adventure and romance, *Wilson*, a history lesson fraught with controversy, was not everybody's idea of what constituted entertainment. Zanuck believed, probably correctly, that his film failed in cities like Minneapolis, St. Paul, Kansas City, Denver, Cleveland, and St. Louis because of the native conservatism of many regions of the country where the seeds of isolationism persistently grew and the support for international organization was not as vigorous. In October of 1944 Zanuck brought a print back to his hometown of Wahoo, Nebraska, for a special showing which the entire town attended. In nearby Omaha the *Wilson* premiere was sold out. The next day only 75 people out of a population of a quarter million came to the theater. "Why should they pay seventy-five cents to see Wilson on the screen," asked Zanuck's old family doctor, succinctly explaining the regional antipathy, "when they wouldn't pay ten cents to see him alive?" Although it was among the highest grossing films of the year, by the end of its national run it registered a net loss of two million dollars.[37]

Another disappointment befell Zanuck and his associates. *Wilson* was nominated for ten Academy Awards, including best picture of the year. Of all the nominees on "Oscar Night" in March 1945, the real contest was between *Wilson* and *Going My Way*, an enormously popular and sentimental film, also nominated for ten awards. *Wilson* won a total of five for editing, sound recording, interior decoration, cinematography, and screen

---

to Wilson, Jan. 9, 1945, Baker Papers; *Life and Letters*, "Potomac Edition" (New York: Scribner's, 1946), vol. 1, xviii; Mrs. Margaret Maher of Doubleday's Inventory Control Office and Mrs. Maria Noreika of Scribner's Reference Department kindly provided comparative sales statistics.

[37] Zanuck to Sweetser, Nov. 7, 1944, Sweetser Papers; Frederick W. Williams, "Regional Attitudes on International Cooperation," *Public Opinion Quarterly* (Spring 1945), 49. (Records of box office receipts for *Wilson* are no longer available at Twentieth Century-Fox; my estimate is based on 33 reports published in *Motion Picture Daily* from Aug. 3 to Dec. 22, 1944, and in *Motion Picture Herald*, Oct. 26, 1944, 48.) Gussow, *Don't Say Yes*, 119–120; *Time*, June 12, 1950, 65.

writing, before the last three categories were named. But King the director, Knox the actor, and *Wilson* the film lost to Leo McCarey, Bing Crosby, and *Going My Way.* Zanuck was mortified. He remained unswerving in his belief in the film and its subject. He donated $5,000 toward the purchase of the new Wilson Foundation headquarters and later $50,000, in Mrs. Wilson's name, for the restoration of Wilson's birthplace in Staunton, Virginia. *Wilson* was listed on the *New York Times'* annual Ten Best list and Alexander Knox's performance was voted the best of the year in a national poll of newspaper, magazine, and radio film reviewers. Nonetheless, Zanuck was embittered. Three years later, while accepting the 1947 best picture citation for *Gentleman's Agreement*, he glared at the Academy gathering and said, "Many thanks, but I should have won it for *Wilson.*" He has never changed his mind.[38]

After the ordeal of *Wilson*, Twentieth Century-Fox shied away from any further expensive experiments and abandoned Zanuck's plans to produce a film based on Willkie's *One World* as a kind of internationalist sequel to *Wilson.* The Wilson Foundation published a special booklet about the critical reception to the film and proposed that it be shown annually in theaters throughout the world. Shelved away for years after 1946, the film was never to be re-released until the 1960s when it was circulated on television in a truncated black and white version.

Wilson is one of the unique film biographies in American popular culture. Like its subject, ironically, its ascendance was as spectacular as its ultimate failure. Yet, the film is a noteworthy celluloid reflection of the past generation, revealing contemporary attitudes toward the problems of peace and war, as well as toward Wilson and his era. In an ostentatious but tasteful manner *Wilson* attempted to remind Americans of the global responsibilities they once shirked but would have to accept in a new, postwar world. Woodrow Wilson, who won the war, ironically gained increased fame for a lost peace. Therein lies his great personal tragedy, and, perhaps to some extent, therein lies his greatness. In the most recent major study of Wilson, Lord Patrick Devlin wrote of Wilson and his abortive world mission: "He is and will always be historically great because he was the first to try."[39] Much the same might be said of Zanuck's special experiment, despite its artistic shortcomings, because of what his film singularly tried to do.

In the thirty-odd years since *Wilson's* first exhibition historians have rendered a more balanced, realistic judgment of the subject. They have ex-

[38] Robert Osborne, *Academy Awards Illustrated* (Los Angeles: ESE, 1966), 122 and 128–29; Alden Hatch, *Edith Bolling Wilson* (New York: Dodd, Mead, 1960), 270; *New York Times,* Jan. 9, 1946, 21; Gussow, *Don't Say Yes,* 120.
[39] Lord Patrick Devlin, *Too Proud to Fight: Woodrow Wilson's Neutrality* (New York: Oxford Univ. Press, 1975), 679.

plored more critically the internal and external forces which motivated him and have exposed the numerous chinks in the idealistic Wilsonian armor. Although the motion picture is marred by many oversights and gloss, it is basically an honest film, commendable in its intent, inspiring in the ideals it professed. Its overview of Woodrow Wilson is not at variance with that of any of the President's most respected biographers—from Baker to Link—for their works have in part been predicated upon the principle of doing honor to the memory of a great man. Countless ambitious historical spectacles have been produced since *Wilson*. But because of the nature of the moment, none of them have flashed their history as imposingly as *Wilson*—if only for awhile—or told so many stories at the same time, generated so much praise and controversy, and spurred so many passionate expectations.*

*I am grateful to Professors Andrew Buni, Janet Wilson James, and R. Alan Lawson of Boston College, and Professor Jack T. Kirby of Miami University (Ohio), and to M. Francesca Nudo and my aunt, Dorothea M. Knock, whose encouragement and critical suggestions made it possible for me to complete this essay. An uncut 35mm. Technicolor print of *Wilson* is available at the UCLA Film Archives. All photos are courtesy of the Museum of Modern Art, Film Stills Archive, 21 W. 53rd Street, New York City.

TRADITION AND DIPLOMATIC TALENT: THE CASE OF THE COLD WARRIORS

BRUCE KUKLICK

Sometime in the early 1970s the "Cold War," in its classical ideological and rhetorical form, ended, its place in the American consciousness pre-empted by the United States' failure in South Vietnam and the Watergate scandals. Policy makers involved in detente and in the repercussions of intelligence agencies run amuck gave up the ghost of monolithic communism. The spectre that had haunted Americans—of malevolent foreign leaders challenging their freedom—vanished when confronted by the Nixon White House; the challenge might come instead from their own leaders. In this sense the Cold War was no longer contemporary history; it had truly receded into our past, perhaps to be summoned up in the future as a guide or warning but no longer to be master of the international stage. This essay examines the historical guides and warnings that now defunct diplomats did summon up at the time when the Cold War itself was front and center; it explores the historical consciousness decision-makers had of their undertakings during the arduous quarter century succeeding World War II, the way statesmen's awareness of the past sustained and warranted action, and gave it moral significance. Diplomats contended that the past taught them appropriate behavior. They believed that their responses to the rigors of the forties, fifties, and sixties were informed by lessons from the immediately preceding period. I examine this usable past and how officials used it.

Like members of other communities, diplomats worked within a tradition, a set of beliefs that have proven their ability to order the experience of a given cultural constituency. An operative tradition provides a community with criteria to distinguish one activity from another, establishes priorities among activities, and enables the community to perform whatever activities make it a community at all. Insofar as the tradition has a socially grounded organizational function, it will also include institutions and prescribed norms of conduct; but I here emphasize only the historical justifications for action instilled among diplomats because of their collective sense of the recent past. Their vision included a general orientation to the history of the United States in the early twentieth century and the way in which its diplomacy fit into the global politics of nineteenth-century Europe. The beliefs also embraced more focused and historically located ideas about international relations: specific analogies and heuristic maxims designed to meet present and future problems on the basis of past experience. Indeed, insofar as diplomacy is uncertain, the tradition served to present uncertainties as a series of "problems" that it solved; the tradition validated itself by transforming the contingency of experience into something subject to maximum control. The successive solving of problems added to the richness of the tradition, and each solved problem itself took its place in the tradition, later illustrating how problems of a certain kind had been handled. Of course, the more able a tradition is to expand and adapt—its organizing devices flexible enough to preserve it through temporal changes—the more likely it is to command the loyalty of its constituency. But flexibility must be balanced by a willingness to maintain a tradition's fundamental truths, to protect the integrity of the tradition itself. This demand requires adherence to home truths, something almost like dogma, and dogma—if such it be—was also part of the post–World War II diplomatic repertoire.[1]

*   *   *

Although I shall be concerned with U.S. diplomatic history after World War II, the policy makers' past begins before this and draws especially on the history of American foreign relations from 1917 to 1941. Indeed, the experience of World War I is so essential to post–World War II diplomats that I shall call their view Wilsonian. The substance and history of Woodrow Wilson's diplomacy do not require retelling here, but there are a few elements that have defined its operative meaning for those directing Amer-

[1] For a more theoretical discussion of these issues see David A. Hollinger, "T. S. Kuhn's Theory of Science, and Its Implications for History," *American Historical Review,* 78 (1973), esp. p. 373; and my own uncontrolled "History as a Way of Learning," *American Quarterly,* 22 (Fall 1970), 609–28, from which parts of the present article have been excerpted.

ican foreign affairs after 1941: internationalism, interventionism, and collective security.[2]

Before World War II, however, many influential decision makers were not adherents of this Wilsonian perspective. Although studies have shown that we cannot describe interwar diplomacy as isolationist, neither can we describe it as Wilsonian.[3] But during this period many who were later to make policy proclaimed their allegiance to it. Most importantly, Cordell Hull, a young congressman in 1917, became zealously committed to Wilson.[4] When Hull became Secretary of State in 1933, he surrounded himself with likeminded individuals. Norman H. Davis held the unique rank of Ambassador at Large in the first years of the New Deal; he was Hull's closest confidant and shared the Secretary's comprehension of international matters.[5] Breckinridge Long, who assumed many positions of diplomatic prestige in the thirties and early forties, was another of Hull's intimate friends. Long was proud to have kept the "faith of Woodrow Wilson" after World War I; it was the "motivating thought of my political life for about thirty years."[6] George Messersmith, a highly regarded and perceptive career diplomat, also made Hull's commitments his own. He was in "complete accord" with the Secretary "on all fundamental problems affecting our foreign relations."[7] William Dodd, Ambassador to Germany from 1933 to 1938, was "utterly loyal" to Hull's ideals.[8] Undersecretary of State Sumner Welles, often personally at odds with Hull, never doubted his chief's diplomatic outlook; Welles "believed passionately in the ideals

[2] Good sources for this interpretation of the past are: Wolfgang Friedmann, "Interventionism, Liberalism, and Power-Politics: The Unfinished Revolution in International Thinking," *Political Science Quarterly*, 83 (1968), 169–89; and A. Michael Washburn, "The New Generation Dissents," and Willard H. Mitchell, "The Great Transition," published together in *Walt Rostow, Vietnam, and the Future Tasks of American Foreign Policy* by the Center of International Studies (Princeton, 1967). Rostow's important lecture, "The Great Transition: Tasks of the First and Second Postwar Generations," originally published in *The Department of State Bulletin*, 56, no. 1448 (March 27, 1967), 491–504, is reprinted as an appendix to these two essays, and I have cited Rostow from it.

[3] See, for example, William Appleman Williams, "The Legend of Isolationism in the 1920s," *Science and Society*, 18 (Winter 1954), 1–20.

[4] Cordell Hull, *Memoirs*, 2 vols. (New York: Macmillan, 1948), vol. 1, 69, 81–85, 107, 133–34.

[5] Robert A. Divine, *The Illusion of Neutrality* (Chicago: Univ. of Chicago Press, 1962), 42.

[6] Fred L. Israel, ed., *The War Diary of Breckinridge Long* (Lincoln, Neb.: Univ. of Nebraska Press, 1966), 332–33, 392.

[7] George Messersmith Papers, University of Delaware, Box III, Correspondence 1944, Folder C., Messersmith to Hull, November 27, 1944.

[8] Quoted in C. C. Tansill, *Back Door to War* (Chicago: H. Regnery, 1952), 341–42.

of Woodrow Wilson." One historian has written that at the beginning of the war he was "the most eloquent prophet of the new world order."[9]

Throughout the twenties and thirties, high tariff protectionism, the Depression, or "isolationism" always hampered the objectives of Hull and his associates. But whatever the status of Wilsonian precepts prior to 1941, Pearl Harbor signaled the end of effective opposition to this orientation. After American entry into the war, the set of premises defining Wilsonian policies became dominant not only among policy makers but also with the Congress and the public. Robert A. Divine, a student of recent American diplomacy, has argued that in 1945 few feared a repetition of the tragedy of World War I. After the Japanese attack, "internationalists" set out to convince the American people that their refusal to join the League of Nations had led to World War II. By 1945, Divine contends, these internationalists had overwhelming support. "Looking to the past rather than to the future, they tried to learn from the mistakes of an earlier generation."[10] Reflecting on the past in his *Memoirs,* Hull took a similar position: "I was in Congress during the war that taught us the interrelationship of the continents, though the lesson went unheeded. I conducted our foreign relations, under the President, in the war that proved to us all the need for a world organization to prevent further wars."[11] In his radio address of December 8, 1941, Franklin Roosevelt delivered this message to his listeners:

> In these past few years—and, most violently, in the past few days—we have learned a terrible lesson. It is our obligation to our dead—it is our sacred obligation to their children and our children—that we must never forget what we have learned.[12]

Few would deny that Wilson's views triumphed after World War II, nor that the policy decisions of the postwar period increasingly depended on a Wilsonian rationale. Only after the consolidation of this consensus does it become appropriate to speak of Wilsonianism in my sense. The constellation of premises out of which policy developed after 1945 did contain peculiar large-scale beliefs about international affairs, models for diplomatic behavior, and specific maxims or analogies to govern conduct. It also contained exemplars—shared problem solutions and standard initia-

[9] Robert A. Divine, *Second Chance* (New York: John Wiley, 1967), 42. This book contains a wealth of material on the points I have tried to make in this paragraph.

[10] Divine, *Second Chance,* 4.

[11] Hull, *Memoirs,* vol. 2, 1729.

[12] Quoted in Basil Rauch, *Roosevelt, from Munich to Pearl Harbor* (New York: Creative Age Press, 1950), 494. See Rauch's remarks on the speech and those of John E. Wiltz, in *From Isolation to War, 1931–1941* (New York: Crowell, 1968), 3.

tory experiments. Three elements of this matrix deserve investigation. The first is the context of European history into which more specific beliefs about U.S. history fit; the second, an understanding of Wilson's failure with the League of Nations; the third, a set of commitments about what may be broadly named "lessons of the thirties."[13]

Former Secretary of State Dean Acheson wrote at greatest length on the Wilsonian view of the larger historical context out of which postwar policy sprung. As early as 1939 Acheson praised the European diplomacy of the nineteenth century (1815–1914). The economic and political system in existence at that time, Acheson observed, had collapsed with World War I, and attempts to restore it had not succeeded; American diplomacy had to take an effective part in trying to re-create it.[14] Acheson often came back to this opinion in later years. The destruction of the Concert of Europe and the thirty year interregnum that followed 1914 meant that leadership in the restoration of world order must come from the United States.[15]

Acheson was certainly not alone in summoning up the ghosts of Castlereagh and Talleyrand. FDR called European politics to mind in this respect as did his secretary of war, Henry L. Stimson. Eugene V. Rostow took a similar tack as early as 1945 and repeated it in defending policy in Vietnam. American diplomacy, Rostow claimed, rested "on the tradition of concerted Great Power action to prevent or to confine war. The tradition has been developing, through a series of hopeful trials and tragic errors at least since 1812. In the last century, a concert of Great Powers managed to preserve a tolerably secure system that prevented the possibility of major successful aggression." Since World War II, he urged, the

---

[13] There are, of course, many historians who share the paradigm I attribute to policy makers, but I am here only concerned with the beliefs of the amateurs and not the professionals. Almost a year before Pearl Harbor, Roosevelt had touched on all these elements in his famous "Arsenal of Democracy" speech, reprinted in *The Puritan Ethic in United States Foreign Policy,* ed. David L. Larson (Princeton: D. Van Nostrand, 1966), esp. 198–200.

[14] "An American Attitude Toward Foreign Affairs," Address delivered at Yale University, November 28, 1939, mimeograph, Yale University Library, 2–6. The address was inserted into the Senate record when Acheson was nominated as secretary of state in 1949 and was reprinted in the first volume of his autobiography. See *Pattern of Responsibility,* ed. McGeorge Bundy (Boston: Houghton Mifflin, 1952), 6–7; and Dean Acheson, *Morning and Noon* (Boston: Houghton Mifflin, 1965), 267–78.

[15] Dean Acheson, *Power and Diplomacy* (Cambridge, Mass.: Harvard Univ. Press, 1958), 3, 69; and his 1954 article written for *The New York Times,* " 'Instant Retaliation': The Debate Continued," reprinted in *American Foreign Policy Since 1945,* ed. Robert Divine (Chicago: Quadrangle, 1969), 93. See also *Present at the Creation* (New York: W. W. Norton, 1969), 3–8.

United States had sought to build a new system.[16] Even Lyndon Johnson lectured the American public in the *Reader's Digest* on these large themes in European history. After describing nineteenth-century diplomacy in the usual fashion, Johnson argued that in not recognizing our stake in rebuilding the European system after World War I, we were "prisoners of our past"; after 1945, however, we attempted to rebuild an orderly system.[17]

Both Rostow and LBJ used a more specific precedent that occupied a prominent place in policy makers' history: the role of Wilson and the League of Nations. Johnson contended that in 1920 "we rejected Woodrow Wilson's advice and tried to crawl back into the 19th century." Rostow made the same appraisal and additionally blamed FDR for not preventing World War II by leading the United States into the League of Nations in the mid-thirties.[18]

The belief that American presence in the League would have prevented the conflict of 1939 was a critical one in the diplomatic inventory of valuable historical experiences. On Armistice Day of 1941 Sumner Welles made a speech at Wilson's tomb and reminded his audience of Wilson's prediction that if the U.S. rejected the League, the next generation would fight a second world war. Roosevelt made the same causal connection between the American response to the League and the coming of World War II. Stimson, too, believed this to be "the great lesson" of World War I. The failure of the United States to support Wilson was the "greatest error" made by America in the twentieth century: "The penalty of this error was visited upon the nation and the world in later events." The surrender of Germany and Japan gave Wilson's diplomacy even greater significance. James Byrnes, secretary of state from 1945 to 1947, recalled Wilson's domestic political problems in an extended manner, hoping that American policy makers would never again repeat Wilson's mistakes. While he was still undersecretary, Acheson also urged that history had made a

[16] For Roosevelt see footnote 13; for Stimson, see Henry L. Stimson and McGeorge Bundy, *On Active Service in War and Peace* (New York: Harper, 1948), 591–92; for Rostow's earlier view, his "American Security and Foreign Economic Policy," *Yale Review*, N.S. 34 (1945), 495–523; the later view is expressed in his *Law, Power, and the Pursuit of Peace* (Lincoln, Neb.: Univ. of Nebraska Press, 1968), 40, 118–19. His brother, Walt Whitman Rostow, made these claims in a more generalized manner in a 1946 address, "The American Diplomatic Revolution," Oxford Inaugural Lecture (Oxford, England, 1946).

[17] "In Quest of Peace," *Reader's Digest* (February 1969), 224, 226–27.

[18] Johnson, "In Quest of Peace," 224; E. V. Rostow, *Law, Power, and the Pursuit of Peace*, 33, 97. See also John Kennedy's remarks in his *The Strategy of Peace*, ed. Allan Nevins (New York: Harper and Row, 1960), 193, 202.

"good try" at repeating itself in 1945.[19] President Truman made much
of these grave lessons in 1947:

> After the First World War, the United States proposed a League of Nations,
> an organization to maintain order in the world. But when our proposal
> was accepted and the League was established, this country failed to become
> a member. Can any thoughtful person fail to realize today what that mistake
> cost this nation and cost the world? This time we are taking a different
> course.[20]

Perhaps the historical analyses that proved most potent in determin-
ing the responses of American policy makers since the Depression were
those to which I have given the label "lessons of the thirties." In a significant defense of American conduct of foreign affairs from 1945 to the
late sixties, Walt Whitman Rostow, special assistant to former President
Johnson, made this point explicitly. Rostow declared that postwar security
policy was rooted in a consciousness of a "tragic common failure to stop
aggression in time during the 1930's"; "we recall often the lessons of the
1930's."[21] Whatever this last phrase denoted in the exact circumstances
in which it was used, it was popularized in the historical rhetoric of American diplomats. During the 1962 Cuban crisis President Kennedy reminded his countrymen: "The 1930's taught us a clear lesson: aggressive
conduct, if allowed to go unchecked and unchallenged, ultimately leads to
war." With respect to South Vietnam, President Johnson asserted in 1965:
"the central lesson of our time is that the appetite of aggression is never
satisfied. To withdraw from one battlefield means only to prepare for
the next."[22]

But the application of historical analogues from the Depression to succeeding events did not originate in the 1960s. In the late forties both

[19] For Welles, see *Second Chance,* 45; for Roosevelt, see Lucius Clay, *Germany and the Fight for Freedom* (Cambridge, Mass.: Harvard Univ. Press, 1950), 7–8, and Willard Range's analysis in *Franklin D. Roosevelt's World Order* (Athens, Ga.: Univ. of Georgia Press, 1959), especially 1–10; for Stimson, see Stimson and Bundy, *On Active Service,* 101, 102, 106; for Byrnes, his *Speaking Frankly* (New York: Harper and Brothers, 1947), 233–36, 243; for Acheson, see the Felix Frankfurter Papers, Library of Congress, Washington, D.C., Box 1, Acheson to Frankfurter, December 19, 1947.

[20] "Peace, Freedom, and World Trade," Address by the President of March 6, 1947, State Department Publication 2789, reprinted from the *Department of State Bulletin* (March 16, 1947), 1–2.

[21] W. Rostow, "The Great Transition," 497, 503. See his brother's remarks in *Law, Power, and the Pursuit of Peace,* 39.

[22] "President Kennedy's Radio-Television Address, October 22, 1962" in *The Cold War: A Book of Documents,* ed. Hans Trefousse (New York: Capricorn, 1966), 278; Lyndon B. Johnson, "Pattern for Peace in Southeast Asia," in Larson, *The Puritan Ethic,* 209. See also Walt Rostow's statement in "The Great Transition," 500.

Truman and Acheson made clear that the United States "must not go through the thirties again." Indeed, the response to world events in the five years after the war indicated that the Americans interpreted the present and future in categories directly derived from the preceding three decades. In his *Memoirs,* Truman urged that the landmarks in American diplomacy —policy in Iran, Greece, Britain, and Korea—were all based on learning from "two calamitous world wars."[23] In 1965, Secretary of State Dean Rusk repeated this evaluation with the benefit of more historical hindsight:

> A clear understanding that it is imperative that aggression not be allowed to succeed produced the Truman Doctrine, a declaration of general policy assisting other free peoples who are defending themselves against external aggressions or threats. It produced our aid to Greece and Turkey and to Western Europe. It produced the Berlin airlift. It produced the North Atlantic Treaty and other defensive alliances of the free world. It produced the historic decision to repel the aggression against the Republic of Korea and the defensive military establishments of the free world. And it produced the decision to assist the peoples of Southeast Asia to preserve their independence.[24]

By far the most popular way of expressing these governing historical formulations was to use the noun "appeasement." In *War or Peace,* a 1950 analysis of recent American diplomacy, future Secretary of State John Foster Dulles devoted an entire chapter to appeasement; he proclaimed that the United States policy of "no appeasement" had been born at the September 1945 Foreign Minister Conference at which Secretary Byrnes presided. In commenting on Dulles, Byrnes himself recalled his disappointment at this conference and his report to the American people that "the United States does not believe in agreement at any price." At the same time, Naval Secretary James Forrestal, later to become the first secretary of defense, urged that appeasement had not worked with Hitler and would not work with the Soviet Union.[25] When Dwight Eisenhower

[23] The quotes are Truman's from "Peace, Freedom, and World Trade," 5, and from his *Memoirs* (Garden City: Doubleday, 1956), II, 464; see also pp. 340, 346. For Acheson, see *Pattern of Responsibility,* 62, 69; and "The Joint Defense of Western Europe," Statements by the Secretary, et al., February 15 and 16, 1951, Department of State Publication 4126 (Washington, D.C., 1951), 6. See, in addition, Clay's report on the 1948 Berlin crisis in *Germany and the Fight for Freedom,* 44.

[24] Dean Rusk, "Some Fundamentals of American Policy," in Larson, *The Puritan Ethic,* 171. In later apologies for American policy, both of the Rostow brothers drew Rusk's parallel. See E. V. Rostow, *Law, Power, and the Pursuit of Peace,* 14, 15, 67; and W. Rostow, "The Great Transition," 500, 503–04.

[25] John Foster Dulles, *War or Peace* (New York: Macmillian, 1950), 24–32, 127; James F. Byrnes, *All in One Lifetime* (New York: Harper, 1958), 312; James Forrestal, *The Forrestal Diaries,* ed. Walter Millis (New York: Viking Press, 1951), 96.

made his famous "I shall go to Korea" speech in October 1951, he also drew on this interpretation of the past. Although he would bring a just and speedy end to the war, Eisenhower promised that he would "always reject appeasement"; it was not the road to peace but "surrender on the installment plan." Nine years later presidential nominee Kennedy also conjured up the vision of a policy of appeasement as the greatest mistake.[26]

So popular did appeasement become as a means of encapsulating and stigmatizing certain policies that it often resulted in vicious name-calling within the governing elite itself. Dulles took it for granted that he could adequately describe FDR's wartime alliance with Russia as appeasement. Whether it could be justified as a wartime measure Dulles thought to be a controversial question, but Senator Arthur Vandenberg, the important Republican spokesman for foreign affairs in the forties, was already thankful in April of 1945 that "FDR's appeasement is over." By early 1946, however, Secretary Byrnes was complaining of Vandenberg's and Dulles' charges of appeasement. At the same time important members of Byrnes' own party made the same accusation. Both Averell Harriman, ambassador to the Soviet Union, and presidential chief of staff, William Leahy, felt Byrnes' policy that of an appeaser. Slightly over a year later, Harriman argued from a different perspective that any conciliatory moves toward Russia were always "construed as appeasement" rather than the implementation of a sincere desire to work together.[27]

By the late forties, concern for Democratic "appeasement" had grown apace. Although Dean Acheson had to answer charges that he had been an appeaser, they seemed "so incredible" that he could not believe that "even disinterested malevolence could think them up."[28] When Douglas MacArthur was unceremoniously stripped of his command in Korea in 1951, he responded in his "Old Soldiers Never Die" speech with a thinly disguised attack on the administration. He could only deprecate those who could appease Red China; they were "blind to history's clear lesson." Shortly thereafter, Omar Bradley, head of the Joint Chiefs of Staff, defended policy. American action was not appeasement, but "a militarily sound course of action under the present circumstances."[29]

[26] *The Truman Administration: A Documentary History,* eds. Barton J. Bernstein and Allen J. Matusow (New York: Harper and Row, 1966), 486; Kennedy, *Strategy of Peace,* 218.

[27] Dulles, *War or Peace,* 25; Bernstein and Matusow, *The Truman Administration,* 159, 212–14; Forrestal, *Diaries,* 132, 288; William Leahy Diary, Library of Congress, Washington, D.C., December 26, 1945; January 1 and February 26, 1946.

[28] Bundy, ed., *Pattern of Responsibility,* 6, 24–26.

[29] Bernstein and Matusow, *The Truman Administration,* 468–80.

This evidence and much more that is available abundantly document what is perhaps an obvious thesis: that the historical knowledge of the diplomatic community revolved around a small number of continuously articulated interpretations. It is also clear that they in some way guided diplomatic behavior for a quarter century. But in addition to the meaning attributed to the Concert of Europe and America's role in the twentieth-century world and to that attributed to Wilson, the League of Nations, and what I called "lessons of the thirties," there is a lesson of the thirties that merits special attention. While this structure of beliefs, models, and maxims was important to the tradition, British diplomacy at Munich was crucial. The interpretation placed upon Munich functioned as a negative exemplar, the central and outstanding example of how *not* to conduct business. The "consequences" of Munich had been shared by all those responsible for the conduct of foreign relations, and provided a common conception of how they ought—or ought not—execute policy. In back of the statements concerning the teachings of the two wars, the aggression of the thirties, appeasement, and peace at any price was the vision of Neville Chamberlain returning from his conference with Hitler. Analogizing a situation to Munich was a sacred act, and its implications seemingly so devastating that its full glory was reserved for times of national crisis. That Munich led to war was a dogma believed by all those who had been initiated in the practice of diplomacy, and its explication was almost ritualistic in the defense of policy.

In June of 1950, when President Truman announced to the nation the existence of war in Korea, he crystallized the American commitment unmistakably: "We will not engage in appeasement," he said; "The world learned from Munich that security cannot be bought by appeasement." Describing the administration's attitude toward sending troops to Korea, McGeorge Bundy declared, "It had avoided the feeling of helpless shame which is associated with the name of Munich, and even in the darker days of the first withdrawal there was a recognition that defeat would be less painful than inaction would have been." When questioned on the defense of Berlin and West Germany in 1960, John Kennedy implied that he regarded the matter with utmost seriousness:

> If we took the view which some Englishmen took, that Prague or the Sudetendeutsch were not worth a war in '38—if we took that view about Berlin my judgment is that the West Berliners would pass into the Communist orbit, and our position in West Germany and our relations with West Germany would receive a fatal blow. . . . They're fighting for New

York and Paris when they struggle over Berlin. Therefore, I think we'd
have to make it cold—and mean it—that we would fight.[30]

Diplomats within this tradition claimed to have learned. When a child
touches a hot stove, he conducts a low level experiment. The generaliza-
tion—if one touches a hot stove, one will be burned—need usually be
tested only once. The child alters his behavior so that he is not put into
the position of being burnt again; he has learned. Prior to both World
Wars, diplomats believed that the United States attempted to avoid international commitments; it need not or would not act in concert with
other powers when an "aggressor" threatened stability. By 1945 the
United States had been "twice burned," and Americans had to alter their
behavior. Policy makers acted, so they believed, to avoid the catastrophes
of 1917 and 1941. This goal entailed United States intervention if someone challenged world peace and order. There were to be no more Munichs.
In effect, after World War II American diplomats "solved" recurring
problems by working through the tradition. Problems were *in fact* problems
because they were significant within a Wilsonian framework. As policy
makers compared the twenty years of diplomacy after World War II with
the history that preceded it, they could surely agree that Wilsonianism
worked. Policy objectives were achieved, and without the wars crucial
to the development of their tradition, diplomats resolved the crises that
gave it birth. Similarly, when the tradition came under attack in the late
sixties and finally unravelled, diplomats responded predictably in its defense.

The *Washington Post* journalists covering the 1967 march on the
Pentagon wrote that among all the demonstrators ran the conviction that
Vietnam was "an old man's war," caused by another generation's
commitments to the military system.[31] As *New York Times* columnist Tom

---

[30] "War in Korea," in *American Diplomacy and the Sense of Destiny,* vol. 4, *War
and Challenge, 1942–1966,* eds. Perry E. Gianakos and Albert Karson (Belmont,
Calif.: Wadsworth Publishing Co., 1966), 62; Bundy, ed., *Pattern of Responsibility,*
253–54; Kennedy, *Strategy of Peace,* 213; see also Trefousse, ed., *The Cold War,*
260, 263. The Munich Analogy is an extraordinary phenomenon. Witness Noam
Chomsky's use: "As Munich showed, a powerful and aggressive nation with a
fanatic belief in its manifest destiny will regard each victory, each extension of its
power and authority as a prelude to the next step. . . . Herein lies the danger of
appeasement, as the Chinese tirelessly point out to the Soviet Union, which they
claim is playing Chamberlain to our Hitler in Vietnam," ("The Responsibility of Intellectuals," in *The Dissenting Academy* [New York: Pantheon, 1968], 285). The Analogy
has also been used in comic strips (see "Steve Canyon," by Milton Caniff in *The New
Haven Register,* July 28, 1969), and in the movies (see the scene in *The Godfather* where
Michael Corleone is being instructed on how to kill his father's enemies).

[31] *The Washington Post,* October 24, 1967.

Wicker commented, "A generation is coming to maturity as surely shaped in reaction to Lyndon Johnson's war as he or any other American had been shaped in reaction to dust bowl, Depression, and World War II."[32]

If the tradition was attacked, however, its attackers did not initially go unchallenged. Dean Acheson, the historical *doyen* of American diplomatists, had no intention of writing his massive *Present at the Creation* in 1964. But in the years intervening between then and the 1969 publication of his apology for his years in the State Department, Acheson changed his mind. He decided to write because, since 1964, the country and "particularly its young people" had come "to a mood of depression, disillusion, and withdrawal from the effort to affect the world around us."[33] Walt Rostow also explicitly acknowledged that distinctive sets of commitments shaped the behavior of sixties policy makers and that of the "younger generation." Some of the young believed, Rostow remarked, that the American government was "old-fashioned" in its approach. and he admitted that the Johnson Administration, at least, often recalled experiences "not part of the living memory of those now in the universities." Nevertheless, despite his commitment, Rostow also saw the war as a crucial point of periodization. He believed that Vietnam might be the last great confrontation of the postwar era, the closing of one chapter in modern history and the opening of another; if the Cuban missile crisis was the Gettysburg of the Cold War—the time at which alien forces were put on the defensive—then, he maintained, Vietnam could be the Wilderness. A potential Munich was transformed into the testing ground for ultimate victory.[34]

Other officials did not respond to criticism with Rostow's grace, but the crisis did create a need for historical justification which stridently and repeatedly returned to the most emotion-laden argument, the Munich Analogy. Facing an older audience composed of the U.S. Council of the International Chamber of Commerce in March of 1965, Secretary Rusk lectured on Vietnam:

> So what is our stake? What is our commitment in that situation? Can those of us in this room forget the lesson that we had in this issue of war and peace when it was only 10 years from the seizure of Manchuria to Pearl Harbor; about 2 years from the seizure of Czechoslovakia to the outbreak of World

[32] *New York Times Magazine* (August 24, 1969), 90.

[33] I use the word "apology" because Acheson wrote that "detachment and objectivity" seemed to him less important than telling a tale "of large conception, great achievements, and some failures." Acheson, *Present at the Creation*, "Apologia Pro Libre Hoc," xvii; see also his second thoughts in an interview in the *New York Times Book Review* (October 12, 1969), 2.

[34] W. Rostow, "The Great Transition," 503–04.

War II in Western Europe? Don't you remember the hopes expressed in those days: that perhaps the aggressor will be satisfied by this next bite, and perhaps he will be quiet. Remember that? You remember that we thought that we could put our Military Establishment on short rations. . . . We learned that, by postponing the issue, we made the result more terrible, the holocaust more dreadful. We cannot forget that experience.[35]

Five months later the President took up this theme: "If we are driven from the field in Vietnam, then no nation can ever again have the same confidence in American promises. . . . We learned from Hitler at Munich that success only feeds the appetite of aggression."[36]

Toward the end of 1967, inspired by the Pentagon march, a stream of historical statements unsuccessfully sought a rationale for American activity. In October Vice President Hubert Humphrey delivered an emotional, sarcastic attack on dissenters. "I have not forgotten the lessons of the '30s," Humphrey said, "when men cried 'peace', and failed a generation." The next day Rusk again warned that the ideas of protestors were those of the appeasers of Hitler. Although told that his politics of the 1940s and 1950s were out of date, Rusk proclaimed that the new politics of the 1960s did not differ from those of the 1930s: they "led my generation to the catastrophe of World War II."[37]

In their post-election defense of repudiated policy, President Johnson and his secretary of state interpreted the matter in apocalyptic terms. In defending his lack of rhetorical ability, Johnson drew a comparison between himself and Winston Churchill. Even Churchill's eloquence, Johnson wrote, had not enabled the Englishman to get a hearing until his country was in mortal danger. Had Churchill come to power earlier and given credence to a "domino" theory, he would have suffered political defeat. In a sober evaluation of the past and future, Rusk also despaired of those "who want to abandon our commitments" around the world. He worried because he saw "the first signs on the horizon" of a return to isolationism.[38]

Of course, no single crisis destroys a tradition. Moreover, critics within a community—in this case men like Townsend Hoopes and McGeorge Bundy—are far more destructive than a disaffected generation of youth, although the latter do much to *create* critics. President Nixon defended *his*

---

[35] Rusk, "Fundamentals of American Policy," 173 in Larson, *The Puritan Ethic.*
[36] Johnson is quoted from Howard Zinn's "Munich, Dominos, and Containment," in *Vietnam: The Logic of Withdrawal* (Boston: Beacon Press, 1967), 85. See also Johnson's "Pattern for Peace in Southeast Asia," 208–10, 212–13.
[37] *The Washington Post,* October 24, 25, 1967. A month later, the President reiterated these claims. *The Washington Post* (December 5, 1967).
[38] Johnson, "In Quest of Peace," 250; *New York Times,* March 3, 1969.

Vietnam policy just as Rusk had,[39] and his spokesman, Vice President Spiro Agnew, later fought the 1972 campaign against George McGovern by predicting that the Democrat would be worse than Neville Chamberlain at Munich.[40] But Vietnam was an *experimentum crucis* in which the tradition was found wanting. Thereafter, it would fade away, its demise occurring slowly as its adherents died off, as the problems it picked out ceased to be relevant, and as younger officials incorporated its viable aspects into a new synthesis of beliefs. When Dean Rusk returned to Washington to testify before a congressional committee in the middle of 1972, he enunciated historical views identical to those he had repeated in the sixties, but he acknowledged that his ideas made him sound like a man "from another age."[41]

*   *   *

The rise and decline of a tradition of diplomatic ideology illustrates in one period what Karl Marx wrote about so eloquently:

> Men make their own history, but they do not make it just as they please; they do not make it under circumstances chosen by themselves, but under circumstances directly encountered, given and transmitted from the past. The tradition of all the dead generations weighs like a nightmare on the brain of the living. And just when they seem engaged in revolutionizing themselves and things in creating something that has never yet existed, precisely in such periods of revolutionary crisis they anxiously conjure up the spirits of the past to their service and borrow from them names, battle cries and costumes in order to present the new scene of world history in this time-honoured disguise and this borrowed language.[42]

Nonetheless, I have not asked and have not tried to answer the important Marxist question of social theory: what is the relation between this ideology and actual diplomatic practice? Most American historians have taken the uncritical position that diplomats have said what they have meant. On the one hand, however, such flatfooted gullibility need not result in a defense of American diplomacy. In studying learning behavior in children, Jerome Bruner has developed the concept of "preemptive metaphor." Pressures of various sorts on children may sometimes

[39] *New York Times,* March 13, 1971.

[40] Ibid., July 1, 1972.

[41] Ibid., June 29, 1972.

[42] *The Eighteenth Brumaire of Louis Bonaparte* (New York: International Publishers, 1963), 15.

produce a narrowing of their ability to learn, but they still retain some of the learning achievements acquired earlier. In these cases their behavior is for a time defined by a principle of cognitive organization, which ties disparate material together by a common fear and a common avoidance, a primitive early achievement. When children guide their action by a preemptive metaphor, they conceive every potentially disruptive or harmful situation in terms of its "limitless" quality. As long as the metaphor's requirements dominate the children's perspective—"not missing anything dangerous lest one be overwhelmed by it"—it is difficult to treat new material and tasks in their own terms, free of the compelling context to which they have been assigned. Bruner argues that the functioning of a preemptive metaphor amounts to the rule of those cognitive operations that prevail in the absence of conscious control; in fact, it appears to be the hallmark of such unawareness. In the absence of conscious or "logical" checks, the metaphor may grow by a "cancerous metastasis," and make it almost impossible for children to substitute coping for defending; so much of their world may be implicated as potentially dangerous that they are truly crippled.[43]

Bruner also takes up these themes in his discussion of the various procedures that test the "validity" of learning categories. The test of "affective congruence," Bruner urges, makes categorizing dependent on a feeling of subjective certainty or even necessity. In the pure case, affective congruence is defined by an unjustifiable intuitive leap buttressed by a sense of unshakeable conviction. Consistency with other categorizations or acceptance by a reference group may also help to validate categorizations whose prime support comes from affective congruence, but their essential quality is the feeling of subjective certainty accompanying them. Categories associated with this peculiar type of validation seem to be inaccessible to disproof in proportion to the strength of the inner needs they fulfill. As Bruner puts it, "because they are particularly inaccessible to disproof, [they] are of special interest to the student of non-rational behavior."[44]

It is not difficult to see that a psycho-historian could accept what the diplomats said at face value and, using Bruner's insights, condemn their actions. In fact, on this account their behavior would be, literally, crazy, as it was, for example, in the signal case of James Forrestal. This interpretation would also gain plausibility if the analyst were to consider the

[43] Paraphrased from *On Knowing* (Cambridge, Mass.: Harvard Univ. Press, 1949), 12–15; and *Toward a Theory of Instruction* (Cambridge, Mass.: Harvard Univ. Press, 1966), 130–47.

[44] Bruner, et al., *A Study of Thinking* (New York: Wiley, 1956), 17–21.

personality of the man Henry Kissinger described as the "meatball" President, Richard Nixon.

On the other hand, to be credulous about the assertions of diplomats is not necessarily to accuse them of insincerity. The critical problem is to credit their sincerity but simultaneously to link their utterances to the operative policies that defined American diplomacy from World War II to Vietnam—neo-imperialism, global expansionism, the explosion of military spending, the support of reaction around the world, and the growth of clandestine intelligence agencies. The question is not so much: Did they say what they meant? but: What did they mean when they said what they said?

Contributors

THOMAS J. KNOCK is a doctoral candidate at Princeton University. He is currently working as a research assistant to Professor Arthur S. Link on the Papers of Woodrow Wilson.

BRUCE KUKLICK, Professor of History at the University of Pennsylvania, is most recently the author of *The Rise of American Philosophy: Cambridge, Massachusetts, 1860–1930* (1977).

JOHN P. MCWILLIAMS, JR., Associate Professor of American Literature at Middlebury College, is the author of *Political Justice in a Republic: Fenimore Cooper's America* (1972) and of numerous articles on American literature and history.

THOMAS H. PAULY is Associate Professor of American Literature at the University of Delaware, specializing in the nineteenth century. He has also published a number of articles on American popular culture and on film.

THOMAS P. RIGGIO is Assistant Professor of English at the University of Connecticut (Storrs). He has published numerous articles and reviews, and is the editor of the forthcoming Dreiser autobiography, *Dawn,* part of the definitive Dreiser Edition. He is a specialist in American Studies.

RICHARD M. ROLLINS, Assistant Professor of History and American Studies at Carroll College, is the author of several articles and reviews in various scholarly journals. His essay on Noah Webster is part of a full-length intellectual biography now in press. He is currently preparing a study on the historiography of early national America.

JOAN SHELLEY RUBIN, currently Assistant Professor of History at the University of Western Ontario, has previously taught at Yale University and McMaster University. Her essay in this volume is a revised excerpt from a forthcoming book on Constance Rourke.

LEILA ZENDERLAND is a doctoral candidate in American Civilization at the University of Pennsylvania. Her interests are in social science history and she is currently working on a biography of Henry Herbert Goddard. She has been managing editor of *American Quarterly* since 1974.

DATE			
OCT 2 5 1979